POLITICAL *and* MILITARY SOCIOLOGY

POLITICAL *and* MILITARY SOCIOLOGY

Democracy, Security, and Armed Forces

AN ANNUAL REVIEW,
VOLUME 44

Neovi M. Karakatsanis
Jonathan Swarts
editors

Routledge
Taylor & Francis Group
LONDON AND NEW YORK

First published 2016 by Transaction Publishers

Published 2017 by Routledge
2 Park Square, Milton Park, Abingdon, Oxon OX14 4RN
711 Third Avenue, New York, NY 10017, USA

Routledge is an imprint of the Taylor & Francis Group, an informa business

ISSN: 0047-2697
ISBN 13: 978-1-4128-6426-8 (pbk)

Contents

Volume 44, 2016

Introduction

Jonathan Swarts
Neovi M. Karakatsanis
Editors

This volume encompasses a diversity of empirical research on topics that are related by their focus on security, military training and culture, and the challenges of bureaucracy, law, and violence in affecting the quality of democracy. The five articles in this volume also cover an impressive geographic range—from Europe (Greece) to Africa (Zimbabwe and Nigeria) and the Middle East (Iraq).

The volume begins with two essays that address the challenges posed to democratic polities by corrupt and inefficient bureaucratic and legal institutions, on the one hand, and by electoral violence and intimidation, on the other. The first, by Constantine P. Danopoulos, argues that the rule of law is the most important feature of high-quality democratic governance. However, the rule of law and its accompanying benefits must be based on supportive elements of a country's political culture. His analysis of Greece, however, shows that a dualistic political culture there inhibits the impartial rule of law and encourages such phenomena as nepotism, corruption, inefficiency, lax law enforcement, and the avoidance of merit. Calling for substantial cultural change, he argues that such a shift is necessary to improve the quality of Greek democracy.

The second article in this volume addresses the quality of democracy in Nigeria—and specifically the threat to it posed by the violent actions of student fraternities. For this article, Ifeanyi Ezeonu interviewed 30 individuals from an institution he calls the "University of the South." He argues that, in Nigeria, influential politicians have closely integrated ties with a number of student fraternities—organizations of which many politicians are alumni. These fraternities, while ostensibly intended to provide mutual support to students and graduates, actually are deeply enmeshed in a symbiotic relationship with politicians, furthering their aims through violence, intimidation, and harassment of their political opponents—something done by all sides of politics with impunity. The result, Ezeonu argues, is a serious threat to the proper functioning of Nigerian democracy.

Two articles then address the security and military challenges in present-day Iraq. In the first, Remi M. Hajjar examines how military advisors define success in difficult, unconventional missions. Using the case of US military advisors in Iraq, and utilizing a multimethod analysis that employs US and Iraqi documents and personal interviews, he argues that advisors often work to a somewhat subjective standard of "good enough," and many consider success to be when they have completed "working themselves out of a job." In this process, he contends, successful military advisors must resemble a Swiss Army knife, playing such multiple roles as peacekeeper-diplomat, warrior, and subject matter expert.

A second article on Iraq tackles the problems faced by the troubled security sector there. Based on interviews and other research in Iraq, Andreas Krieg analyzes the Maliki regime and its failure to provide for the security of all Iraqi citizens. He argues that the clientelistic, kinship-based, and sectarian approach of the government in attempting to "coup proof" the regime has created a vacuum of security for the country's non-Shia population. With the state failing in its fundamental responsibility to provide security for the entire population, unprotected groups are now a source of willing recruits to organizations such as ISIS promising such protection.

The final essay analyzes the acculturation of new soldiers to military life through the training experiences of Zimbabwean recruits. A former Zimbabwe Army soldier himself, Godfrey Maringira uses in-depth personal interviews with fellow soldiers to explore the acculturation and resocialization processes undergone by new military recruits in their basic training. Using Foucauldian ideas of discipline and punishment and Goffman's work on "total institutions," he describes the key features of basic military training in the recruit's transition from the civilian to a military mentality. In so doing, he emphasizes the importance of military hierarchy, the orders of one's superiors, and techniques of discipline and control.

Finally, as is customary for *Political and Military Sociology*, some of the most current and topical recent book publications are also reviewed in the book review section.

In Memoriam:
George A. Kourvetaris

Late in 2015, George Kourvetaris, the founder of the *Journal of Political and Military Sociology* (*JPMS*), the predecessor of this series, passed away at the age of 81. Born in Greece in 1933, he emigrated to the United States as a young man. He encountered numerous challenges as he worked his way through college (a story told with charm and verve in his memoir, *Sharing My Life's Journey*), receiving his PhD from Northwestern University in 1969 and becoming Professor of Sociology at Northern Illinois University. His passion for scholarship and the academic life resulted, among many other accomplishments, in the founding of *JPMS* in 1973, at the time the only such journal in existence. For over 30 years, he guided the *JPMS* into a position of prominence, along the way publishing the work of both established figures as well as that of the innumerable rising young scholars who benefitted from his kindness and support. Seeing the *Journal* transition to *Political and Military Sociology: An Annual Review* in 2010 was not easy for George, yet he recognized its necessity in order to keep what was, in many ways, his life's work alive. It was our honor to be entrusted with his legacy and even more to call him a mentor and friend. It is to Professor George A. Kourvetaris, with thanks, respect, and warm affection that we dedicate this volume.

Neovi M. Karakatsanis
Jonathan Swarts

A central figure in the creation and publication of the *Journal of Political and Military Sociology* was Betty A. Dobratz, now Professor of Sociology at Iowa State University. She graciously provided the following reflection.

George Andrew Kourvetaris, Professor Emeritus of Sociology at Northern Illinois University (NIU) and founder of the *Journal of Political and Military Sociology* (*JPMS*), died October 20, 2015. He was my mentor while I was a graduate student, his research assistant at Northern Illinois University, and assistant editor of *JPMS* for numerous years. In the early 1970s, he asked me to search for any journals that combined both political and military sociology. I thought perhaps he had an article in mind to submit to such a journal, but I could not find any such publication. To fill the void and stress the intersectionality of politics and the military, he then founded *JPMS* with limited institutional support but great determination and passion. In addition he demonstrated the entrepreneurial spirit that he wrote about in his academic work about Greeks and Greek Americans. He introduced special guest editors and topics in *JPMS* on a variety of political and military issues that generated great interest in both fields. He received numerous academic awards for his achievements during his lifetime, including one from the political sociology section of the American Sociological Association for his editorship of *JPMS*. Like me, I am sure that he was very thankful that part of his academic legacy continues in the form of this annual publication.

Betty A. Dobratz

Cultural Attributes and Legal
"No-Man's-Land" in Greece

Constantine P. Danopoulos
San José State University

Political and Military Sociology: An Annual Review, 2016, Vol. 44: 3–24.

The main thrust of this study is to advance and substantiate the argument that elements of Greek culture are responsible for the poor state of law implementation and enforcement in the country. The rule of law is arguably the most indispensable condition for the emergence and maintenance of quality democratic governance. The cultural dualism that permeates Greek society promotes nepotism, in-group collectivism, laxness toward the rule of law, excessive legalism, short-time horizons, avoidance of merit, and a host of other values and attitudes that influence the behavior and orientations of the nation's bureaucratic and law enforcement structures. These bodies reflect the collectivity's general values, beliefs, and orientations.

Few would disagree that the rule of law is of paramount importance to democracy and quality democratic governance. Juan Linz and Alfred Stepan (1996: 10), for instance, deem it as an "indispensable condition" (1996: 10), while Guillermo O'Donnell believes that "the rule of law is among the essential pillars upon which any high quality of democracy rests" (2005: 3). Larry Diamond and Leonardo Morlino are equally assertive, stating that "the rule of law is the base upon which every dimension of democratic quality rests" (2005: xv). Succinctly stated, the rule of law means that there is a clear, understood, stable, and self-sustaining body of law based on universally accepted principles and precepts. It is not retroactive, treats all citizens equally regardless of class, economic status, gender, color or creed, and it is applied fairly, evenly, and consistently across a broad network of judicial and law enforcement systems, including the courts, bureaucracy, the police, and other law enforcement bodies.

Though indispensable, enacting a law is of little importance unless the law is implemented; and "passage is not the same thing as implementation" (Channel 2006: 145). In other words, the legislative adoption stage must be followed by the public policy or policy implementation and enforcement stages. Implementation "is that set of activities directed toward putting a program into effect" (Jones 1984: 166), and enforcement refers to the legally constituted bodies assigned the task of discovering, deterring, rehabilitating, or punishing persons who violate the rules, values, and norms permeating a community. Implementation and enforcement bodies provide the organizational structure, interpret and translate the often arcane language of the law into tangible and efficacious policy goals, apply or provide the intended services or rewards, collect payments, exact fines, or implement other forms of punishment. In Larry N. Gerston's apt analogy, implementation and enforcement agencies "are like the contractors who put into place the plans drawn by the architect" (2002: 113).

But like enactment, implementation and enforcement of laws do not take place in a sterile, watertight and airtight atmosphere, but in an environment where cultural norms, values, and attitudes play a major, but not always visible, role. A seasoned observer reminds us that "law is not just the sum of courts, legislatures, police, prosecutors, and other formal institutions with some direct connection to law. Law is also a normative system that resides in the minds of the citizens of a society" (Carothers 2006: 20). Echoing these sentiments, another experienced practitioner notes that often "resistance to implementation comes from cultural predispositions, not some technical failure of implementing and supporting institutions" (Channel 2006: 148). Diamond and Morlino concur, stating that "diffuse" and unsupportive cultural attitudes undermine the quality and sustainability of the democratic rule of law (2005: xvi). Lawrence Whitehead conveys a similar message when he states,

> However fair and thorough the justice system, only a small and unrepresentative set of cases can be attended to. For the great majority of acts by individual citizens the rule of law is only enforced to the extent that groups and individuals practice appropriate forms of self-limitation. The rights and restraints of citizenship are thus internalized rather than imposed. (2002: 166)

Being part of the same social milieu, bureaucrats and other implementation and enforcement officials cannot help but be influenced by the prevailing cultural norms and beliefs of the larger society. As B. Guy Peters correctly asserts, the "very general value orientations in the society will influence the behavior of individuals working in formal organizations, as well as the manner in which those organizations are structured and managed." And he adds that "despite the seemingly abstract nature of cultural boundaries on behavior, governments and individual civil servants can violate prevailing [societal] norms only at their risk" (2010: 34–36).

By all accounts, law implementation in Greece is very weak, and this is at the very heart of the country's past and current economic difficulties. A study conducted on behalf of the European Union (EU) places Greece at the bottom of the scale as far as law implementation and enforcement is concerned. Nearly half of the laws passed never reach the implementations stage—a barely passing grade even on the most lenient grading scale (*Kathimerini* 2007). This is corroborated by the World Bank's *Worldwide Governance Indicators* report[1] and a host of academic studies (see, for example, Mitsopoulos and Pelagidis 2011; Kalyvas, Pagoulatos and Tsoukas 2012).

Although lack of law implementation and enforcement in Greece (and elsewhere) is a complex process involving a multitude of variables, nevertheless culture is undoubtedly a salient factor. This article will seek to analyze the connection between culture and the travails of law in the Greek context. The study will begin with a discussion of the nature and idiosyncrasies of culture in modern Greece and will be followed by analyses of the processes and difficulties associated with law implementation and enforcement in the country.

Cultural Imperatives

Culture is an elusive and often controversial subject; as such, it lends itself to different definitions ranging from thick descriptions to more practical or subjective ones. Advancing a more encompassing approach, Clifford Geertz views culture as "a system of inherited conceptions expressed in symbolic forms by means of which people communicate, perpetuate, and develop their knowledge about and attitudes toward life" (Geertz 1973: 89). Samuel P. Huntington favors a narrower or practical perspective—one that sees culture "as values, attitudes, beliefs, orientations, and underlying assumptions prevalent among people of a society" (Huntington 2000: xv). The GLOBE research project settles for a more middle of the road view. The study defines culture as "a set of relatively stable, basic, and shared practices and values that help human social groups or societies find solutions to two basic fundamental problems: how to survive, grow, and adapt to the environment (external adaptations), [and] internal integration that permits daily functioning and ensures the capacity to adapt and survive" (Hartog 2004: 401).

Despite differences, the various definitions agree that culture is learned by growing up in a society; its main elements are shared by members of the collectivity; and it profoundly affects the thoughts, actions, and feelings of everyone in society. Three functions of culture are viewed as most salient. First, culture supplies people with the skills needed to adapt to their surroundings. Second, as the basis of social life, culture provides norms, values, expectations, attitudes, and other forms of knowledge that "allow people to cooperate with one another, live in families and other kinds of groups, relate to members of their own and opposite sex, and establish political and legal systems" (Bailey and Peoples 1999: 24). And third, culture affects people's perception of reality; establishes the belief system through which they "perceive, interpret, analyze, and explain" developments around them; and "provides a filter or a screen" that affects their view of the world (Bailey and Peoples 1999: 24–25). In Eugene Hunn's epigrammatic phrase, "culture is what one must know to act effectively in one's environment" (quoted in Patterson 2000: 208).

What are the major elements of Greek culture? In what is by far the most perceptive work on the subject, P. Nikiforos Diamandouros attributes Greece's rough and largely unsuccessful road to modernization on "cultural dualism" (πολιτισμικός δυϊσμός) by which he refers to two parallel, competing, and equally strong cultural tradition currents permeating the country's society: the older, traditional, or underdog and the younger or reformist.[2] Spread in much of the Balkan Peninsula, the older of the two has deep roots in the Balkan-Ottoman legacy and is profoundly influenced by Orthodox cosmology, which harbors long and often militant antiwestern sentiments. The traditionalist cultural current is characterized by a pronounced introversion, a protectionist and paternalistic state, ambivalence toward market capitalism and an uncomfortable view toward innovation, parochial and even primordial attachments, a penchant for populism, and "latent" authoritarian orientations and a preference for "sultanistic" regimes.

These general features were further shaped and refined by prevailing national norms and experiences. Greece emerged from the war of independence a small, weak, and economically feeble entity with limited or "conditional sovereignty." To improve this dismal position, and with the acquiescence—if not outright encouragement—of the Orthodox Church, the country's leaders embraced and pursued a policy of irredentism aimed to liberate and incorporate lands once held by the Byzantine Empire. The pursuit of this policy—known as the national project (Μεγάλη Ιδέα)—exacerbated and deepened dependency on foreign powers, divided the country's political landscape, and resulted in a number of military– and foreign policy–humiliating defeats. These national and often traumatic experiences, augmented by the prevailing traditional cultural features, formed the backdrop and the point of reference of the traditional cultural current in Greece. As such, the oldest of the country's cultures is characterized by (a) a siege mentality and a pronounced proclivity toward conspiratorial explanations of events, both domestic and international; (b) a culturally anchored, pervasive, exaggerated, yet quite insecure and fragile, sense of nationalism; (c) a tendency to see the world in Manichean terms: that is, the forces of light that support Hellenism, on the one hand, and its detractors, on the other; (d) an exaggerated sense of Greece's importance in the world and its contribution to the development of western civilization, touted to mask a feeling of cultural inferiority toward the west; and, finally, (e) a pronounced tendency to identify and sympathize with groups or individuals perceived to have been mistreated by the domineering west.

As might be expected, these salient tenets of the traditionalist culture affected its perception of democracy and the role of the state. Augmented by the very nature of legal positivism, which views the state as the sole source of law and individual rights, the traditionalist culture elevates the state to a predominant position vis-à-vis civil society. Its perception of democracy and politics is ambivalent. The traditionalist culture (a) prefers direct and unmediated exercise of power and finds limited use for institutions as mediators between the individual and the state; (b) has an ambiguous, if not resentful, view of the importance of civil society; (c) shows a clear and pronounced preference for small and familial structures as the best means to promote and protect clientelistic practices; (d) adheres to a formalistic, rather than substantive, view of the democratic process; and (e) sees politics as an instrument to advance such perceptions. The traditionalist culture is arguably the majority view, and its strength derives from the less affluent segments of the Greek society, including small farmers and people with less than average education.

The younger or reformist culture is smaller in number but tends to be stronger among the more dynamic sectors of society. It draws its support from people with diasporic connections, entrepreneurs with international experiences, and those with more than average education. Unlike the traditionalists who look for inspiration within the confines of the region, the reformers look west and draw intellectual energy from the philosophical heritage of the Ancient Greeks, the spirit of the Enlightenment, and the achievements of liberalism. The reformers advocate a market economy; the development of a secular state along west European lines; an institutionalized, rather than direct, exercise of state power; a vibrant civil society to restrain the state; and a broad and encompassing, rather than restrictive, conceptualization of individual rights. To realize their vision of a modern, democratic, and stable Greece, the proponents of the reformist culture (a) favor quick adaptation to change; (b) are open to currents and ideas emanating from Western Europe; (c) support cultural and other links to foster a cosmopolitan orientation; (d) champion a secularly anchored, milder, more sophisticated, and less strident nationalism; (e) are mindful of the country's relative weakness in international affairs and advocate a measured, realistic, and prudent Greek foreign policy; and (f) feel that their success surviving in various and often difficult environments abroad should serve as a symbol that can benefit the country.

Support for the two cultural traditions cuts across social classes, regional, and even ideological lines. Yet, they have existed in the same environment and, as such, have been influenced by each other; however, neither has managed to achieve supremacy. While both have experienced peaks and valleys, nevertheless they have exhibited strong survival and entrenchment instincts. On a larger scale, the two currents have "imparted conflictual logics on social and political interactions and have commensurably impeded the emergence of alternative, consensual, and more integrative arrangements capable of acting as effective mechanisms of interest representation or aggregation in the country" (Diamandouros 1994: 32). Diamandouros postulates that Greece's membership in the EU is likely to have a catalytic effect on the country's cultural dualism that will lead to the eventual dominance of the reformist culture. The current economic crisis seems not to bear out his prediction, and the traditionalist tendency appears to have gained ground among major elements of the population.

The discussion on cultural dualism helps us trace and identify key elements in Greek culture that negatively affect the rule of law. Utilizing data and a framework for analysis included in a voluminous study, a recent article established the connection between culture and pervasive corruption in the country. The study concluded that, among others, Greek culture is characterized by resistance to change, tolerance for rule-breaking and socially damaging behavior, short-time horizon, spontaneity, tendency to ignore warning signals, weak proclivity toward planning and future orientation, feeble civil society, penchant for in-group (or amoral familism) and self-interest promotion (as opposed to societal collectivism), aggressive discourse, avoidance of merit and preference for leisurely and polychromic life, limited class mobility, excessive legalism and tolerance for corruption and nepotism, excessive legalism and lax attitudes toward even application of the law, and weak capacity and willingness to imagine future contingencies and formu-late strategies that would meet future orientations (Danopoulos 2014). Other studies corroborate some of these points. For example, Dimitri Sotiropoulos questions Greek society's willingness to "accept significant change" (2012: 26), while Kevin Featherstone and Dimitri Sotiropoulos report the country ranks last among OECD countries in "reform capacity" (2013: 33).

The Travails of Implementation

As known, the burden of law implementation rests mainly on the shoulders of the bureaucracy. By its very nature, however, implemen-tation is an intricate process involving society, the bureaucracy, as well as the attitudes of the political class and the quality of laws. For implementation to succeed, society has to be fairly united with respect to its fundamental orientations; trust between the citizens, government, and the bureaucracy must exist. In addition, interagency cooperation, merit, bureaucratic professionalism, and participation in the drafting of laws, as well as supportive cultural attitudes regarding the importance of and fair application of the laws, are also necessary. Moreover, the body of law that the bureaucracy is called upon to implement and soci-ety to accept must be parsimonious, devoid of legalism, clear, stable, nonretroactive, fair, and intended to help govern society, rather than a fig leaf for inaction and nebulous intentions. Very few, if any, of these essentials are present in the Greek context, and it should come as no surprise that law and policy implementation in the country is fraught with pervasive and deep-seated difficulties—nearly half of the laws are never implemented.

The ambivalent attitudes and behavior on the part of the citizens and the state itself have deep and profound cultural roots and do little to engender trust. In terms of structure and appearance, the contem-porary Greek state meets all the criteria associated with democratic governance and the rule of law, but it does not appear to trust its citi-zens to act responsibly. Feeling insecure, the Greek state goes out of its way to dominate civil society. It passes laws that it does not intend to implement or implements unfairly; it rails against corruption but practices it to hilt; and while loudly affirming its commitment to individual rights, it fails to protect minorities and those at the bottom of the socioeconomic pyramid. In return, since the state does not trust its citizens, Greek citizens have no reason to be trusting toward the state. Indeed, citizens feel ambivalent toward their state; they need it and yearn to render their support, but they do not fully trust its intentions and capacity to deliver on its promises or to behave as a responsible and worthy custodian of their interests.

In the three decades following the demise of the colonels' dictatorship (1974–2005), the Greek state has enacted about 3,500 laws and regulations, 18,500 presidential decrees, and over 200,000 ministerial decisions (Makridimitris 2006: 240). Legal hyperinflation is a basic but substantial part of the problem, and it is connected to the polarized nature of the party system, which leads to the insidious proclivity to see politics as a zero-sum game. Instead of seeing governance as a continuing process where the new party in power seeks to improve on the record of their predecessors, the leaders of each new government dismiss everything their predecessors did as completely wrongheaded and proclaim the need to start from the ground up. This vicious cycle does little to provide continuity and stability or to engender citizen trust, which is an indispensable ingredient in the rule of law.[3] Such practices can be dismissed as political hyperbole, yet words have consequences and serve to undermine the very foundation upon which trust in government rests.

When they come to power, governments take advantage of the relative weakness of parliament, concoct, and ram through the legislative assembly reams of laws in a thinly veiled exercise intended to create the illusion that they are cleaning the mess they inherited and, therefore, fulfilling their electoral promises. But many of the bills passed are simply ornamental laws with little or no intention of ever being implemented. Lawmaking, then, is frequently used as an alibi to create the appearance of action and, as such, to muddy the water and to mask the failure to keep promises. The problem is compounded by the myriad of ministerial decisions and directives as well as regulations issued by national and local government bodies. The flurry of ministerial directives is particularly intense in the initial stages of a minister's tenure in office, which sometimes lasts for only a year or less. These tactics provide government officials and majority members of parliament with talking points and ammunition to placate and deflect criticism from the opposition or the mass media. Fred W. Riggs terms such practices as "double talk" and views this type of lawmaking or rulemaking as "prismatic." In his words,

> prismatic is a law which provides for one policy although in practice a different policy prevails. A rule is formally announced but is not effectively enforced. The formalistic appearance of the rule contrasts with its actual administration—officials are free to make choices, enforcing or disregarding the rule at will. . . . Apparent rules mask without guiding actual choices (1964: 201).

Since they are intended for atmospherics and not necessarily for implementation, ornament laws and many ministerial directives are not carefully crafted and frequently contradict laws in force. Yet, they become part of the country's body of law. This deeply flawed and even unethical practice violates the most salient tenets of lawmaking: parsimony, stability, clarity, simplicity, predictability, transparency, and prudential reasons to obey. It creates a nebulous and murky legal environment and opens the doors to violations that harm policy implementation and the rule of law. Interestingly, the government itself is the first to take advantage of the foggy legal landscape and often imposes policies of questionable legality. At the very least, Greek authorities are guilty of opaqueness, deceptive practices, misleading promises, poor coordination, compromising legal stability, and even retroactive application of law.

People are just as quick to fish in the murky legal waters. The well-connected and well-counseled commit punishable offenses but can, and often do, employ provisions in these dormant laws to escape punishment. Moreover, the very existence of ornament laws clogs up the legal system, beleaguers and confuses bureaucrats and law enforcement officials, reinforces public mistrust and cynicism, and encourages deviant behavior. Taken together, these sentiments create a climate that feeds and reinforces a widespread popular belief among Greek citizens that laws are unfair and unevenly selectively applied or not applied at all; hence, skirting the law is both expedient and justified. Put differently, the Greek state produces far more laws and policies than it intends to implement or needs, far more than the nation's bureaucracy and law enforcement institutions can organize and apply, and far beyond what Greek society can comply with, comprehend, and internalize.

But even those laws intended for application are fraught with difficulties that impede implementation, especially as it relates to the first two implementation activities: organization and interpretation. The strict separation between policymaking and administration in Greece gives the bureaucracy little chance to influence the policy implementation process. As such, the group that has the responsibility of turning the law into policy is essentially the one that drafted the law. Apart from a few relevant ministers and some of their top assistants, the organizing group includes a very small number of politically safe "secondment" civil servants and few specialists.[4] Potentially important implementation players, such as representatives from local government and individuals the policy seeks to affect, are largely excluded. One of the early and seminal decisions those who draft the law make is to decide on the allocation of responsibilities. As is typical of many unitary states, the division of labor tends to be horizontal, rather than vertical. That is, ministries are responsible for certain layers of the policy but do not have exclusive responsibility for all of it. For example, paying all expenses is in the hands of the ministry of finance, but procurement is assigned to another agency or ministry.

Once assembled, the organizing group proceeds with the interpretation activity—that is, to turn the law into a set of concrete policies. The composition of the group and the relative influence of the different members are decisive. The nature and texture of the process has several consequences. First, it ensures centralization of decision making in the hands of the political leadership in Athens. Second, by excluding the bureaucracy, the political leadership takes ownership of the policymaking but, at the same time, becomes directly responsible for the policy's successes and failures in all phases, including application. Third, given that the majority of the participants are lawyers schooled in the positivist law tradition—and that often includes the ministers—it is not surprising that the tone of the policy takes a strong legalistic flavor. As a result, policies tend to be written in complex, highly technical language replete with legalistic jargon that tests the skills and knowledge of middle to lower echelon bureaucrats who are called upon to decipher and apply them.

The important role experts can play in translation activities is hampered by three factors. First, there is a noticeable dearth of experts in the Greek civil service. Inadequate pay and the low prestige the bureaucracy enjoys prompt those with talent and specialized skills to seek employment elsewhere. Second, unlike France or Britain, Greece lacks quality public administration institutions of higher learning to train prospective civil servants. For a variety of reasons, recent efforts to establish such schools have not met with much success (Spanou 2001: 106–115). And third, there is shortage of sophisticated and empirically tested literature from which to draw. Greek universities are filled with a plethora of competent academics, but the chaotic and highly politicized institutions of higher learning provide very little opportunity for research and testing of ideas. As a result, experts go into policy implementation meetings armed with the latest in theoretical knowledge, acquired in the course of their studies at top American and European universities, but without having the opportunity to draw on theoretical constructs empirically tested in the Greek context. Instead, they are forced to rely on conclusions extracted from other national settings that may or may not be relevant to the needs, temperament, and norms of a Mediterranean society. Much like lawmaking, the two critical activities surrounding policy implementation (organization and interpretation) do not lead to the formulation of policies that are relevant to the Greek setting and which bureaucrats can comprehend and implement—nor with which the public have sufficient reason to comply.

Application is where the efficacy of policies is tested, and for Greece the record is less than encouraging. Application is inevitably, inseparably, and seamlessly connected to the other two implementation activities. Horizontal allocation of policy responsibilities among various agencies could work well if there were wide and uninhibited coordination between bureaucratic bodies and the flow of information amongst them were continuous and uninterrupted. But the opposite is true in the Greek setting. Owing to the in-group collectivist nature of Greek culture, the level of interagency communication and cooperation in the Greek bureaucratic apparatus is very poor, and the use of the horizontal method tends to aggravate the problem. Each agency goes about implementing its own portion of the policy often oblivious to components of the policy in the hands of other agencies. This leads to compartmentalization of jurisdictions, duplication of efforts, overlapping duties and responsibilities, and lack of accountability. To make matters worse, each agency keeps its own records, does not share them easily with others, and sets its own procedural criteria. As a result, weak coordination is arguably one of the most, if not the most, debilitating impediments plaguing the Greek civil service; it is especially acute at the application level.

Problems emanating from the nature of bureaucratic organization are compounded by the very nature and process of policy interpretation. In-group collectivism prevalent in Greek culture engenders substantial communication difficulties and delays between superordinates and subordinates. Put differently, there are major vertical communication snags and poor planning. Ministries tend to be very slow communicating policy goals, implementation parameters, and guidelines to middle and lower echelon bureaucrats. Implementers are asked to effectuate a policy without having a clear understanding of the specifics of the policy. Similar communication and coordination glitches between the central government and provincial and local governments also hurt policy application to the detriment of public interest.

In addition, the legalistic and often incomprehensible policy statements and directives are a further impediment. This forces bureau managers to request clarification from the ministry. Ministers and other high placed officials respond with scores of additional policy directives aimed at elucidating issues. While directives may clarify one issue, they may end up raising several others, requiring additional clarification. The large volume of follow-up information needed to offer such clarification can add to the difficulty. Tax accountants consistently complain that they have to go online daily to keep abreast of the latest directives from the ministry of finance regarding changes in tax law. The modifications are of such high volume that it is nearly impossible for accountants to track. This situation reaches nearly unmanageable proportions in view of the horizontal, or layer, method of allocating policy responsibilities. Implementers of each layer of the policy are forced go to their superiors for clarification, and the latter issue clarification directives to these subordinates without consulting their counterparts in other layers of the policy implementation process. In the end, different sets of often conflicting application criteria emerge, and citizens are utterly confused and frustrated when having to navigate through an endless and incredibly cumbersome and downgrading labyrinth of offices, which seem incapable of and/or unwilling to provide efficient service.

Greece's bureaucratic apparatus exhibits many/most of the characteristics associated with developing country administration. Such bureaucracies are organized on the basis of imported, rather than indigenous, prototypes; deficiencies in personnel with highly specialized skills, managerial capacity, and technical competence; activities that are oriented toward the realization of often abstract goals, rather than the achievement of specific program objectives, which opens the door to personal expediency preferences, rather than public-principled interests (i.e., subjective rather than objective criteria in policy implementation); openness to exchange services for payments or bribes; large measure of operational autonomy—a characteristic prevalent in countries with a colonial background; and formalism (i.e., policy discrepancies between form and reality).[5] Elaborating on the nature and effects of formalism, Ferrel Heady stresses that formalism is about the gap between expectations and actualities, which decision makers attempt to mask "by enacting laws that cannot be enforced, adopting personnel regulations that are quietly bypassed, [or] announcing a program for delegation of administration discretion while keeping control of the decision-making at the center" (Heady 2001: 302).

The weakness of the bureaucracy in Greece is universally accepted, irrespective of political persuasions, economic status, or background. Analysts cite a number of factors that explain what Sotiropoulos (1996) has dubbed as a colossus with feet of clay. Absence of a rationalist administrative tradition, weak civil society, low pay, lack of prestige, political interference and penetration, and clientelistic practices are some of the many factors. As a result, the lower to middle levels of the Greek bureaucracy are overstaffed with people who possess little training, knowledge, skills, or expertise.[6] Individual pursuits and nepotism abound. Hiring has little to do with need, qualifications or competence; instead, it is connected to the insidious practice of patron-client relations where the political party in power exchanges political support for tenured employment in the civil service.

Similar practices also pervade in the allocation, promotion, and distribution of personnel, which in the Greek bureaucracy are not always executed according to need or workload requirements. As with appointments, political connections and familial preferences tower over public service considerations. As a result, many provincial offices, especially those in more remote parts of the country are seriously understaffed, while others located in Athens or other major cities are often overstaffed. Moreover, such practices have also led to an overabundance (often unneeded) of upper echelon personnel selected on political criteria but a dearth of well-trained professionals in the highest levels of the hierarchy. Commenting on the consequences of this occurrence Calliope Spanou asserts, "Greek administration is characterized by the absence of an administrative elite and failed attempts to create one." In fact, she questions the "extent [to which] there actually is a higher civil service" (2001: 109).

There is little doubt the Greek bureaucracy is politicized, but it lacks expertise, specialized skills, and a clearly defined political mission. Legal hyperinflation and legalism and unclear, confusing, and conflicting policy directives compound the problem. As a consequence, the bureaucracy is neither a key player in any facet of policy implementation nor has the standing, professionalism, or training to prudently and effectively apply the law. Personal or subjective, rather than objective, criteria inform and shape the attitudes of middle- to lower-echelon bureaucrats responsible for policy application. Subjective refers to decision making based on personal connections, kinship, birthplace, or familial ties. The merits of the case or the specifics of the policy tend to be of secondary importance. In other words, the Greek civil service displays many of the characteristics associated with Riggs's "sala" model of administration, by which he means a bureaucracy that is Western/rational in structure and appearance but filled with individuals who employ traditional familial norms, practices, and loyalties (cited in Peters 1989: 42).

Authoritarian behavior, heavy-handedness, disrespect, and rudeness toward the public are readily observable in the halls of the Greek bureaucracy. Civility is sorely absent as well, and without civility, democratic rule of law and quality democracy cannot exist (Whitehead 2002: 74).[7] Needless to say such attitudes and ways of thinking create an environment conducive to favoritism, corruption, graft, and other forms of rent-seeking behavior. *The Global Competitiveness Report 2008–2009* provides evidence supporting favoritism and unfair application of policy (World Economic Forum). Efforts to reform have been rather legalistic, and initiatives to improve the situation have met stiff resistance "from the political-administrative system" (Spanou 2012: 186).

In sum, policy implementation in Greece is fraught with problems in all three implementation-related activities: organization, interpretation, and application. Ornament laws not intended for implementation, poor construction of laws, a weak and deficient bureaucracy, restricted participation in the interpretation activity of implementation, and lack of expertise, specialized knowledge, and adequate communication are some of the ills. Cultural attributes form the backdrop of many of these difficulties. Let us now look at the third stage in the rule of law: enforcement.

Feeble Enforcement

Law enforcement refers to the act of enforcing or ensuring observance of the laws. Some agencies not only engage in parallel implementation and enforcement but also possess the authority and the means to inflict pain in the form of fines and other sanctions to induce compliance. Bodies like the tax collection agency, border patrol, customs, or the city planning and construction inspection bureau can impose sanctions but rely on courts to issue property seizure or incarceration warrants and/or the police to carry them out. The police and highway patrol can issue traffic citations and, under certain circumstances, have the authority to place the violator under temporary incarceration, although court involvement is required for further action.

Like lawmaking and/or policy implementation, enforcement is an intricate, interconnected, interrelated, and often overlapping process involving more than one government agency or bureau. Law enforcement, however, does not stand alone; instead, it takes places in a social milieu and is influenced by the nature of the law as well as the three activities surrounding policy implementation (organization, interpretation, and application).

Unlike their service-providing counterparts, enforcement agencies must determine whether a law has been violated before appropriate measures can be taken. This requires careful examination of the record and frequently involves field inspection. Unclear, contradictory, plethoric, and badly constructed and communicated laws and directives, coupled with inadequacies and inefficiencies in all facets of implementation, form the backdrop against which policy enforcement takes places. Idiosyncratic factors and circumstances in the various law agencies compound the problem and help explain the unfair and uneven enforcement of law. A shortage of qualified and professional bureaucrats is singularly unhelpful, as is a plethora of unqualified, skill-deficient, and merit-lacking personnel.

The police and other domestic security bodies are the quintessential law enforcement agencies. Unlike other law enforcement bodies, security bodies, especially the police, possess the means not just to use coercion in order to enforce the law but to even challenge the government where it is weak and democracy is not well-consolidated. Like other law enforcement bodies, the police must be well-equipped and well-led, properly trained, professional, versed in crime-fighting methods and crowd control, and must enjoy the backing and support of the legitimate political authorities. The objective behind coercion is not to impose compliance by force but, instead, to influence people to select behavior alternatives that result in voluntary compliance with the law. Without clear and clearly communicated policies and laws, adequate resources, a professional ethos, and esprit de corps, as well as sufficient backing by the constitutional authorities, the police will be hard-pressed to enforce the law and may resort to tactics that violate human rights and other dimensions of the democratic rule of law (Kleinfeld 2006: 41).

Though not as problematic as other agencies, the performance of the Greek security forces is less than impressive and appears to have deteriorated in recent years. The chaotic traffic scenes in Athens and other major cities, parked and often abandoned vehicles on sidewalks, shop operators displaying their merchandise in areas designed for pedestrians, and the abundance of unlicensed street venders are a few of the visible signs of lack of law enforcement. In recent years there have been a number of "Rambo- or 007- style" escapes of criminals from maximum security prisons as well as policemen showing up on the scene of a crime without their weapons or behaving in less than a professional manner.[8] Traffic citations issued by police or highway patrol officers are frequently recanted by their superiors, particularly when violators are well-connected individuals. Reports of driver's licenses issued to individuals who never took the test and might not have met the criteria or turning a blind eye on drug dealers and human traffickers are but a few examples of corrupt behavior by Greek security personnel. Finally, there have been numerous instances where security forces beat or abused suspects, especially undocumented migrants.

The crippling economic crisis has hampered the capacity of security forces to enforce the law as well. The rise in unemployment and a general economic tightening have also led to an increase of theft, vandalism, and other forms of criminal behavior. More than half of Greeks have little to no trust in the nation's police and other security bodies. Out of 48 institutions included in a survey, the security forces were ranked twenty-fifth (*Kathimerini* 2008a). Sentiments among the young are less clear but not necessarily encouraging. Slightly less than half of young respondents (44.5%) find the security forces neither trustworthy nor untrustworthy, about 30% see them as trustworthy, and almost 25% as untrustworthy (*Kathimerini* 2008c). As might be expected, the level of apprehension by the country's growing migrant population is even more pronounced, especially among those of Muslim background. Nearly 65% of Muslim migrants state that they do not trust the police, and 80% indicate that they refrain from reporting incidents of maltreatment in the hands of security forces out of fear of reprisals (*To Vema* 2009a)—this in a country that subscribes to international and EU treaties and agreements with respect to human rights and the treatment of migrants and refugees.

Without a doubt, legal hyperinflation and problems associated with policymaking and policy implementation hamper law enforcement. But there are additional factors that impede the performance of Greece's police and other law enforcement bodies. To begin with, there is the issue of numbers and security personnel allocation. Official records indicate that Greece has one of the highest police-population ratios in the EU: one police person for 97–100 people. But if one factors in the number of security personnel assigned to protect politicians, journalists, foreign ambassadors, and other "important" people, the ratio is reduced dramatically to nearly one per 1,000. Wealthy parts of Athens receive better protection than their less affluent counterparts. Residents of high crime areas complain of neglect and lack of protection.

However, other dimensions that relate directly to professionalism, such as personnel allocation, recruitment, and promotion, must also be mentioned. First, there is the issue of office assignments versus field work. Although reliable statistics do not exist, it appears that officers with seniority and experience prefer the office, leaving the field to their junior colleagues. Second, as in other parts of the Greek bureaucracy, nepotism and clientelistic practices play a major role in recruitment and promotion decisions. Third, political, rather than merit, criteria are used to make appointments to leadership positions in the corps as well. Fourth, allocation of responsibilities is not done in a clear and understandable manner. This leads to turf battles between different security agencies, overlaps, gaps, confusing jurisdictions and assignments, as well as lack of trust. Finally, Greek governments are too eager to blame failures on the leadership of security bodies, resulting in frequent dismissals and leadership change. These warp professionalism, harm continuity, and impact negatively on interagency cooperation and sharing of sensitive information, which is of utmost importance in fighting crime and effective law enforcement.

Besides meddling in the security corps' professional interests, Greek authorities do not provide security bodies with proper equipment, sufficient support, and other resources. Owing to the country's centralized system, equipment procurement choices are not always guided by need, feasibility, or quality. Reports of graft involving costly but faulty equipment surface frequently in the press, but little is done to address it. Finally, inadequate compensation forces officers to moonlight to enhance their income. These, plus the difficulties and dangers inherent with law enforcement, damage morale and have had deleterious consequences on officer performance.

Officer preparation is also barely adequate. The training is too short and the curricula of the service academies tend to put greater emphasis on theory than on application. Field training is inadequate and officers are sent to do field work without acceptable levels of physical or emotional preparation. The all too important follow-up training required to familiarize officers with the latest in crime-fighting methods and techniques as well as with the use of new equipment is sporadic and inconsistent. As such, security and law enforcement agencies are steps behind the increasingly sophisticated crime gangs and their accomplices.

Unfortunately, Greek courts also do not have a stellar reputation—neither at present nor in the past. In fact, political influence, if not outright meddling, in judicial matters can be traced all the way back to the inception of the modern Greece state in the late 1820s. The comments of former chief justice V. Kokkinos (1998: 223–237) as well as those of other practitioners and analysts leave little doubt that the Greek judiciary lacks sufficient independence and has sided with the state at the expense of individual rights, regardless of the regime's democratic or authoritarian nature. Adamantia Pollis, for example, avers that "although structurally independent, the [Greek] judiciary has rarely acted as a separate and autonomous branch of government. [Instead], courts have functioned as legitimators of the prevailing regime and bulwarks of the status quo, be it dictatorial or parliamentary" (1987: 596). This attitude has helped foster "a judicial tradition that has been remarkably quiescent vis-à-vis both the legislative and executive branches" (Alivizatos and Diamandouros 1997: 30). Individual protection against government abuses has not been a hallmark of the country's judicial system. As two keen observers correctly note, "in the hands of the judiciary, law has been used more for purposes of state control of society than for protection of individual rights" (Legg and Roberts 1996: 125). Pavlos Eleftheriadis reaches similar conclusions (2007: 150).

Another factor that can undermine judicial independence in positivist law countries is the very structure of the judicial system. The judicial corps is bureaucratic, hierarchical, and professional. As in all bureaucracies, assessment, evaluation, promotion, and advancement are done within the system; a group of senior members selected by those who are up for evaluation are entrusted with the task of assessing and making promotion decisions. This works well in states with a viable tradition of judicial independence and where criteria of merit and performance prevail. However, when such standards are low and governments retain the right to appoint the top judges, an environment is created in which those at the apex of the judicial system have the means to influence lower echelon judges due to the impact the former might have on the latter's career. Under the circumstances, asserts Carlo Guarnieri, "the ability of a bureaucratic judiciary to sustain the rule of law can be questioned" (2003: 239).

Greece's difficulties with establishing judicial independence exemplify the unintended consequences of legal positivism. But idiosyncratic factors complicate the landscape even further. Legal hyperinflation, especially ornament laws, creates a nebulous and cloudy legal environment allowing

Greek judges to adjudicate cases in ways favorable to the well-connected and the well-counseled yet still be within the bounds of the law. At the same time, the cloudy legal landscape prompts Greek citizens to resort to the courts in order to lodge grievances against the intrusive hand of the state. This is exacerbated by the fact that Greece has no clear or recognizable class-action provision forcing would-be litigants to file individual suits. As a result, the legal system is overburdened, and courts are unable to distribute justice in a timely fashion. The comment by a member of the executive body of the nation's judicial servants, Judge K. Kousoulis, is revealing and troublesome: "The distribution of justice in our country is fraught with immense problems. Courts are flooded with hundreds of thousands of cases and cannot respond satisfactorily to the needs of society and provide for fair and timely resolution of disputes" (*To Vema* 2009b).

It should come as no surprise, then, that the public's satisfaction with the Greek judiciary is low. More than one in two Greeks suspects the courts' intentions and questions their commitment to justice (*Kathimerini* 2008b). Among the youth, 32.4% believe that judges are untrustworthy, while 36.6% see them as trustworthy; nearly 40% take a wait-and-see attitude (*Kathimerini* 2008c). A *Eurobarometer* survey finds that 56% of Greeks do not trust the nation's judicial system (*Eleftherotypia* 2009). It goes without saying that such attitudes toward an institution generally regarded as the protector of the underprivileged do not augur well for the rule of law and/or the quality of democracy.

Parting Words

The preceding analysis clearly indicates that elements of Greek culture play a key role in the country's difficulties with respect to law implementation and enforcement, which, in turn, hamper the rule of law and the consolidation of the quality of democracy. Among others, Greek culture is characterized by resistance to change, excessive legalism, tolerance for rule breaking, nepotism, a penchant for in-group collectivism, avoidance of merit, and lax attitudes toward the rule of law. Though not always easy to detect or measure, the country's two parallel and competing cultural traditions create an environment fostering such attitudes. In short, the Greek bureaucracy and the nation's law enforcement apparatus are microcosms of society at large, displaying similar values and orientations.

Cultures, however, are not immutable and can change. Oriental philosophy teaches that crises present not only daunting challenges but also opportunities for self-assessment and renewal. Let us hope that Greece's current and severe economic morass will prove such an opportunity. In Douglass North's words, "[C]hange needs to create new norms of behavior" (quoted in Fairbanks 2000: 279). Greek society desperately needs to reassess many of the prevailing cultural norms and attitudes. Can such deep-seated views and ways of thinking be broken easily? Will the crisis serve as a stimulus for change? Only time will tell.

Notes

1. A summary of the report appeared in *Kathimerini*, 29 June 2009.
2. The discussion on Greek culture is drawn from P. Nikiforos Diamandouros (1994). The work was translated into Greek by Dimitri A. Sotiropoulos under the title, *Politismikos Dyismos kai Politiki Allagi stin Ellada tis Metapolitefsis* (Athens: Alexandreia 2000).
3. Trust is defined as "encapsulated interest," that is, one person's trust in another is typically encapsulated in the second's interest in fulfilling the first person's trust (see Hardin 1998: 9).
4. Secondment refers to a military officer, civil servant, or corporate executive who has been transferred to their post for temporary duty. Occasionally, Greek cabinet ministers pluck a few individuals from the bureaucracy and give them policy making roles. But once in this role, secondments function as advisors to the minister and not representatives of the bureaucracy.
5. The discussion of the characteristics of developing administration is drawn from Heady (2001: 299–302).
6. In fact, there was no data on the number of civil servants employed by the state and only a few years ago the Greek state conducted its first-ever census of state employees.
7. Whitehead (2002: 74) adopts R. G. Collinwood's concept of civility. Collinwood explains that behaving civilly toward someone "means respecting his feelings, abstaining from shocking him, annoying him, frightening him or (briefly) arousing in him any passion or desire which might diminish his self-respect; that is threaten his consciousness of freedom by making him feel that his power of choice is in danger of breaking down and the passion or desire likely to take charge."
8. See, for example, two articles by the daily *To Vema* (2009c) on police involvement (aiding and abetting) in sexual pandering and other forms of crime.

References

Alivizatos, Nikos and P. Nikiforos Diamandouros. 1997. "Politics and the Judiciary in the Greek Transition to Democracy." Pp. 27–60 in A. James McAdams, ed. *Transitional Justice and the Rule of Law in New Democracies.* Notre Dame, IN: University of Notre Dame Press.

Bailey, Garrick and James Peoples. 1999. *Introduction to Cultural Anthropology.* Belmont, CA: West/Wardsworth.

Carothers, Thomas. 2006. "The Problem of Knowledge." Pp. 15–30 in Thomas Carothers, ed. *Promoting the Rule of Law: In Search of Knowledge.* Washington, DC: Carnegie Foundation for International Peace.

Channell, Wade. 2006. "Lessons Not Learned." Pp. 137–160 in Thomas Carothers, ed. *Promoting the Rule of Law: In Search of Knowledge.* Washington, DC: Carnegie Foundation for International Peace.

Danopoulos, Constantine P. 2014. "The Cultural Roots of Corruption in Greece." *Mediterranean Quarterly* 25(2):105–130.

Diamond, Larry and Leonardo Morlino. 2005. "Introduction." Pp. ix-xxvi in Larry Diamond and Leonardo Morlino, eds. *Assessing the Quality of Democracy*. Baltimore, MD: The Johns Hopkins University Press.

Diamandouros, P. Nikiforos. 1994. *Cultural Dualism and Political Change in Post-Authoritarian Greece*. Estudo/Working Paper 1994/50. Madrid: Centro de Estudios Avanzados en Ciencias Sociales, Instituto Juan March de Estudios eInvestigaciones.

Eleftheriadis, Pavlos. 2007. "Syntagmatiki Metarithmisi kai Kratos Dikaiou stin Ellada." Pp. 142–163 in Kevin Featherstone, ed. *Politiki stin Ellada: I Proklisi tou Eksichronismou*. Athens: Ekdoseis Okto.

Eleftherotypia. 2009 (September 10).

Fairbanks, Michael. 2000. "Changing the Mind of Nations: Elements in a Process of Creating prosperity." Pp. 268–281 in Lawrence E. Harrison and Samuel P. Huntington, eds. *Culture Matters: How Values Shape Human Progress*. New York: Basic Books.

Featherstone, Kevin and Dimitri A. Sotiropoulos. 2013. "Assessing Reform Capacity in Greece: Applying Political Economy Perspectives." Pp. 31–46 in Stathis Kalyvas, George Pagoulatos, and Haridimos Tsoukas, eds. *From Stagnation to Forced Adjustment: Reforms in Greece, 1974–2010*. Oxford: Oxford University Press.

Geertz, Clifford. 1973. *The Interpretation of Cultures*. New York: Basic Books.

Gerston, Larry N. 2002. *Policymaking in a Democratic Society: A Guide for Civic Engagement*. Armonk, NY: M.E. Sharpe.

Guarnieri, Carlo. 2003. "Courts as Instruments of Horizontal Accountability: The Case of Latin America." Pp. 223–241in Jose Maria Maraval and Adam Przeworski, eds. *Democracy and the Rule of Law*. Cambridge: Cambridge University Press.

Hardin, Russell. 1998. "Trust in Government." Pp. 9–27 in Valerie Braithwaite and Margaret Levi, eds. *Trust in Governance*. New York: Russell Sage Foundation.

Hartog, Deanne Den. 2004. "Assertiveness." Pp. 395–436 in Robert J. House, Paul J. Hanges, Mansour Javidan, Peter W. Dorfman, and Vilpin Gupta, eds. *Culture, Leadership, and Organizations: The GLOBE Study of 62 Societies*. Thousand Oaks, CA: Sage Publications.

Heady, Ferrel. 2001. *Public Administration—A Comparative Perspective, 6ʰ ed*. New York: Marcel Dekker, Inc.

Huntington, Samuel P. 2000. "Culture Counts." Pp. xiii-xvi in Lawrence E. Harrison and Samuel P. Huntington, eds. *Culture Matters: How Values Shape Human Progress*. New York: Basic Books.

Jones, Charles O. 1984. *An Introduction to the Study of Public Policy, 3ʳᵈ ed*. Monterey, CA: Brooks/Cole Publishing Company.

Kalyvas, Stathis, George Pagoulatos, and Haridimos Tsoukas, eds. 2013. *From Stagnation to Forced Adjustment: Reforms in Greece, 1974–2010*. Oxford: Oxford University Press.

Kathimerini. 2007 (January 21).

Kathimerini. 2008a (December 12).

Kathimerini. 2008b (December 28).

Kathimerini. 2008c (July 27).

Kathimerini. 2009 (June 29).

Kleinfeld, Rachel. 2006. "Competing Definitions of the Rule of Law." Pp. 31–74 in Thomas Carothers, ed. *Promoting the Rule of Law: In Search of Knowledge*. Washington, DC: Carnegie Foundation for International Peace.

Kokkinos, Vasileios. 1998. "O Rolos tis Dikaiosynis stin Antimetopisi tis Diafthoras." Pp. 223–237 in Stephanos Manos, ed. *Kratos kai Diafthora*. Athens: I. Sideris.

Legg, Keith R. and John M. Roberts. 1996. *Modern Greece: A Civilization on the Periphery.* Boulder, CO: Westview Press.

Linz, Juan J. and Alfred Stepan. 1996. *Problems of Democratic Transition and Consolidation: Southern Europe, South America, and Post-Communist Europe.* Baltimore, MD: The Johns Hopkins University Press.

Makridimitris, Antonis. 2006. *Kratos ton Politon: Provlimata Metarithmisis kai Eksichronismou.* Athens: A.A. Livani.

Mitsopoulos, Michael and Theodore Pelagidis. 2011. *Understanding the Crisis in Greece: From Boom to Bust.* Houndsmills, UK: Palgrave Macmillan.

O'Donnell, Guillermo. 2005. "Why the Rule of Law Matters." Pp. 3–17 in Larry Diamond and Leonardo Morlino, eds. *Assessing the Quality of Democracy.* Baltimore, MD: The Johns Hopkins University Press.

Patterson, Orlando. 2000. "Taking Culture Seriously: A Framework and an Afro-American Illustration." Pp. 202–218 in Lawrence E. Harrison and Samuel P. Huntington, eds. *Culture Matters: How Values Shape Human Progress.* New York: Basic Books.

Peters, B. Guy. 1989. *The Politics of Bureaucracy, 3rd ed.* New York: Longman.

Peters, B. Guy. 2010. *The politics of Bureaucracy: An Introduction to Comparative Public Administration, 6th ed.* London and New York: Routledge.

Pollis, Adamantia. 1987. "The State, the Law and Human Rights in Modern Greece." *Human Rights Quarterly* 9(4):587–614.

Riggs, Fred W. 1964. *Administration in Developing Countries: The Theory of Prismatic Society.* Boston, MA: Houghton Mifflin.

Sotiropoulos, Dimitri A. 1993. "A Colossus with Feet of Clay: The State in Post-Authoritarian Greece." Pp. 43–56 in Harry J. Psomiades and Stavros B. Thomadakis, eds. *Greece, the New Europe, and the Changing International Order.* New York: Pella Publishing.

Sotriropoulos, Dimitri A. 1996. *Populism and Bureaucracy: The Case of Greece Under PASOK, 1981–1989.* Notre Dame, IN: University of Notre Dame Press.

Sotiropoulos, Dimitri A. 2013. "The Paradox of Non-Reform in a Reform-Ripe Environment: Lessons from Post-Authoritarian Greece." Pp. 9–30 in Stathis Kalyvas, George Pagoulatos, and Haridimos Tsoukas, eds. *From Stagnation to Forced Adjustment: Reforms in Greece, 1974–2010.* Oxford: Oxford University Press.

Spanou, Calliope. 2001. "(Re)Shaping the Politics-Administration Nexus in Greece: The Decline of a Symbiotic Relationship?" Pp. 101–111 in B. Guy Peters and Jon Pierre, eds., *Politicians, Bureaucrats and Administrative Reform.* London and New York: Routledge.

Spanou, Calliope. 2013. "The Quandary of Administrative Reform: Institutional and Performance Modernization." Pp. 171–194 in Stathis Kalyvas, George Pagoulatos, and Haridimos Tsoukas, eds. *From Stagnation to Forced Adjustment: Reforms in Greece, 1974–2010.* Oxford: Oxford University Press.

To Vema. 2009a (May 31).

To Vema, 2009b (July 5).

To Vema. 2009c (July 9).

Whitehead, Lawrence. 2002. *Democratization: Theory and Experience.* Oxford: Oxford University Press.

World Economic Forum. *The Global Competitiveness Index Analyzer 2008–2009.* Retrieved February 18, 2016 (http://www3.weforum.org/docs/WEF_GlobalCompetitivenessReport_2008–09.pdf).

Violent Fraternities and Garrison Politics in Nigeria's Fourth Republic: Lessons from the "University of the South"

Ifeanyi Ezeonu
Brock University

Political and Military Sociology: An Annual Review, 2016, Vol. 44: 25–50.

This article discusses the co-option of violent student fraternities in the electoral politics of Nigeria's Fourth Republic. The study took place between August and December 2011 at a university in the southern part of Nigeria. For the safety of the research participants, the institution has been given the pseudonym "University of the South." Using ethnographic individual and focus-group interviews from thirty participants from this institution, the study highlights the embedded relationship between politicians and a number of student fraternities in organizing for the capture and exercise of state power. The study concludes that this symbiotic relationship between Nigerian politicians and violent fraternities undermines the development of a democratic political culture in the country.

Introduction

Nigeria has faced a number of public-security challenges since its transition to democratic governance in 1999, which marked the beginning of its Fourth Republic.[1] In the Niger Delta region of the country, a number of ethnic militia groups have fought intermittently for control of the country's petroleum-rich resources. In most southern states, organized criminal groups run some of the most brazen commercial kidnapping[2] syndicates in Africa, and a notorious terrorist group, Boko Haram, has created mayhem in many northern states with the aim of imposing an

Islamic theocracy on the country (Florquin and Berman 2005; Kemedi 2006; Nyiayaana 2011; Osumah and Aghedo 2011; Ezeonu 2014). These forms of security threat tend to attract the greatest attention because of their impact on international oil prices (for instance, the case of the Niger Delta crisis) and the immediate visibility of the horrors they cause. However, an equally serious but often neglected threat has developed from Nigeria's democratic experiment. This threat is associated with the exacerbation of a violent electoral process—conceptualized here as "garrison politics"—in which influential national politicians are implicated (Human Rights Watch 2007; Okolie 2010). It manifests itself in the violent activities of well-armed thugs (or personal "armies") employed by a number of politicians to achieve electoral victory by any means. Many of these thugs are members of student fraternities in the country's tertiary institutions. Other enablers of this garrison politics include the alumni of these fraternities, many of whom are active participants in the politics of the Fourth Republic.

Colloquially known as "secret cults," student fraternities developed into some of the most lethal and potent security challenges in Nigeria in the late 1980s. The oldest of these fraternities, the Pyrates Confraternity, began as an altruistic anticolonial and pan-Nigerian political organization at the University of Ibadan in 1952. The foremost of its founders was Wole Soyinka, Nigeria's celebrated writer and a Nobel laureate in literature. Many years after the establishment of this fraternity, internal disagreements among its members led to a schism and the emergence of rival groups, such as the Buccaneers, the Black Axe Confraternity, the Supreme Vikings Confraternity, and the Eiye Confraternity, among many others. Clusters of these groups exist in most tertiary institutions. These groups are known to terrorize their fellow students and faculty members in pursuit of different parochial objectives. An enduring characteristic of student fraternities in Nigeria is intergroup feuds, which often involve the use of deadly violence and sometimes result in the death of fraternity members, faculty members, and innocent students (Ekpo and Agbo 2005; Rotimi 2005; Eguavoen 2008; Ezeonu 2014). For instance, it is reported that between 1995 and 2004, about 1,743 members of different fraternities were killed in this form of violence (Community Leadership Initiative 2011: 3). Several faculty members were also killed (*Economist* 2008; Ezeonu 2014).

A growing body of work has documented the nature and activities of student fraternities in Nigeria (see Ekpo and Agbo 2005; Rotimi 2005; Ezeonu 2014). This study examines the embedded relationship between politicians and members of student fraternities at an institution given the pseudonym University of the South and discusses its implications for the development of a democratic political culture in Nigeria.

Evidence from this study demonstrates that student fraternities have been incorporated into the country's ruling relations, binding them with the increasingly corrupt and inept national political class. This symbiotic relationship and the culture of impunity which it encourages pose a substantial threat to public security in the institutions concerned and have similarly undermined the development of a democratic culture in the country. The activities of these fraternities and their complicit political class reflect, to some degree, a garrison society in which individuals who control the apparatuses of violence dominate the society (Lasswell 1941) or wield enormous political influence (Firgure and Sives 2002).

Garrison Politics: A Conceptual Framework

The concept of garrison politics developed from the seminal work of Harold D. Lasswell, who predicted a trend in world politics "in which the specialists on violence are the most powerful group in society" and run the apparatuses of the state (1941: 455). In other words, he envisaged a set of political dynamics that favor members of the armed forces as the ultimate wielders of political power. Lasswell's real concern is that "under conditions of continual crisis and perpetual preparedness for total war, every aspect of life would eventually come under the control of the military authorities" (Friedberg 1992: 112). He distinguished this trend from the typical military dictatorships in many non-Western societies by arguing that unlike military dictatorships, "the garrison state" combines "the supremacy of the soldier" with modern (military) technology. As he summed up this construct,

> During emergencies the great powers have given enormous scope to military authority, but temporary acquisitions of authority lack the elements of comparative permanence and acceptance that complete the garrison state. Military dictators in states marginal to the creative centres of Western civilization are not integrated with modern technology; they merely use some of its specific elements (Lasswells 1941: 457).

In other words, Lasswell's concept of the garrison state involves the permanent acquisition and exercise of state power by the military in states with powerful modern military technology. Apparently influenced by the events of the World War II (during which period his paper was published), he raised the prospect of such a transition taking place in militarily powerful states like Japan, Germany, the Soviet Union, and the United States. While Lasswell's social construct has generated a great deal of scholarly attention (Aron 1979; Fitch 1985; Friedberg 1992; Stanley 1996; Dains 2004), political events especially in the militarily powerful states he cites have undermined his prediction. For instance, Friedberg (1992: 113) observes that "even under the intense pressures of its confrontation with the Soviet Union, America did not transform itself into anything resembling a 'garrison state'."

Nevertheless, while the Lasswellian model of the garrison state did not materialize as envisaged in any part of the world, different "specialists on violence" continue to wield enormous political influence and, in collaboration with career politicians, are among the most powerful political actors in many states. In fact, in many parts of the Global South, politicians have often relied on such specialists (including members of the armed forces, the police, and nongovernmental armed groups) to win and/or sustain political power (Figueroa and Sives 2002; Clarke 2006; Human Rights Watch 2007; Levy 2009; Leslie 2010; Okolie 2010).

In many parts of Africa, Latin America, and Asia, members of the armed forces have either exercised direct control of the governments of their respective countries or exerted enormous political influence through their control of the apparatuses of violence. Although these militaries did not fit into the model devised by Lasswell, they exerted immense political influence through the control of the apparatuses of state violence. Contemporary scholars have, therefore, modified the concept of "garrison" politics to accommodate this reality. This alternative version focuses on the expansive influence of violent (usually nongovernmental) groups in the politics of their countries. These groups often act in collaboration with career politicians to achieve parochial political and material objectives (Figueroa and Sives 2002; Sives 2002; Clarke 2006; Omotola 2009). Run-of-the-mill political thugs are not features of garrison politics as they often lack organization and a durable relationship with the politicians they work for. Rather, an enduring relationship between the violent social group and the political actors for whom they work is an important feature of the contemporary understanding of garrison politics.

The trend toward neighborhood-based organized political violence in Jamaica is probably the best known case of this modified construct. Figuroa and Sives (2002) discuss the presence of political "garrisons" in Jamaica as a major feature (and as central to understanding the social character) of that country's national politics. For instance, poor neighbourhoods in Kingston and St. Andrew have over the years served as garrison communities of that country's partisan political divide. In these communities, nongovernmental armed groups (or gangs, as some scholars describe them) receive financial and other political patronage from the country's politicians in exchange for maintaining an almost totalitarian control over the communities' political space (Sives 2002; Clarke 2006). Groups controlling particular garrison communities often use extreme violence to ensure that any opposition to or organization against the dominant party is physically confronted, neutralized, or completely eliminated. In other words, the Jamaican garrison community is "in its extreme form, a totalitarian social space in which the options of its residents are largely controlled" (Figueroa and Sives 2002: 85). This garrison process is associated with a political culture that is tightly controlled by career politicians and their "local enforcers" (Figueroa and Sives 2002: 85–86; see also Clarke 2006).

As modified by contemporary scholars, garrison politics profoundly influences political outcomes in Africa (Human Rights Watch 2007; Okolie 2010). While military dictatorships outside "the creative centres of Western civilization" are not germane to the classical notion of garrison state as conceived by Harold Lasswell, the use of organized violence has historically shaped the praxeological landscape of African politics. This reality evokes the memorable statement of Mao Tse-Tung that "political power grows out of a barrel of a gun" (Tse-Tung 1969: 224). In Nigeria, this was the case for most of its postindependence history. Even as it transitions to democratic politics, another category of violent groups—student fraternities—is stepping into the space created by the political exit of soldiers. As desperate politicians seek to capture or retain state power, these non-governmental armed groups are directly utilized for political support.

Garrison Politics and Democratic Deficit in Nigeria

Political violence has been an enduring characteristic of the Nigerian state, even before independence. During the colonial period, British imperialists relied heavily on state violence to control and govern the various ethnic nationalities they forced into the amorphous political union presently known as Nigeria. The colonialists also used state violence to maximize the economic exploitation of the country, in the process suppressing local opposition to the colonial project. The violent suppressions of the 1929 Aba Women's Riot and the anticolonial agitations of the Zikist Movement were cases in point. Other examples of state violence under British colonialism in Nigeria have been well-documented (Falola 2009). Like their colonial predecessors, the emergent indigenous political leaders at independence also relied heavily on violence to win and retain political power. By the 1964 general election, political violence had become so common and normalized as part of the Nigerian political process that it had started to attract scholarly interest (Dudley 1965).

In January 1966, the military intervened in the country's democracy, in the process killing some key national political actors and complicating not only the feeble democratic experiment but the stability of the Nigerian project itself. The coup leaders were mostly members of the Igbo ethnic group. A countercoup organized by Hausa-Fulani soldiers quickly followed in July of the same year, targeting both Igbo soldiers and civilians across the country. This second coup precipitated two major (and related) violent events: first, a mass killing of people of Igbo ethnic origin in different parts of the country, particularly in the north. It is estimated that at least 30,000 Igbo civilians lost their lives in the violent events that followed this countercoup, in addition to an undocumented number of Igbo military fatalities. Secondly, in the resultant civil war, which lasted for thirty months, it is estimated that at least a million Igbo civilians were either directly massacred by Nigerian soldiers or were starved to death through the Nigerian military government's policy of blockade (Ekwe-Ekwe 2006, 2011; Achebe 2012). These two events represented the first government-sponsored genocide of postindependent Africa. As one Sierra Leonean who lived in Nigeria during this period put it, "the killing of the Igbos has become a state industry in Nigeria" (quoted in Achebe 2012: 82).

Studies demonstrate that most of these killings did not result from military victories achieved at the battlefield but rather from a deliberate and coordinated government strategy to decimate the Igbo population and destroy its economy by targeting the civilian population (see Bird and Ottanelli 2011; Achebe 2012). For instance, in Asaba, an Igbo town at the bank of River Niger, the occupying Nigerian soldiers deliberately massacred about one thousand civilians, specifically targeting men and boys, and savagely raped the female population, including the aged (see Bird and Ottanelli 2011).

In the forty-five years that followed the civil war, Nigeria was mostly under military rule where soldiers ran the apparatuses of the state with impunity, except between 1979 and 1983 (during the period of the Second Republic) and from 1999 until now (the Fourth Republic). The Third Republic which started in late 1991 with elected governments at the state and local levels was quickly terminated by the military junta in June 1993 when the result of a widely acclaimed presidential election was immediately annulled. Generally, the various regimes of the

Nigerian military governments were marked by their callous disregard of fundamental human and civil liberties, as well as disrespect for the democratic ethos. While General Sani Abacha's regime was notorious for its callous suppression of civil liberties and prodemocracy activities, it paled significantly in comparison to that of General Yakubu Gowon, which organized, coordinated, and executed Africa's first postcolonial genocide (Ekwe-Ekwe 2006; Bird and Ottaneli 2011; Achebe 2012).

Regrettably, during the short periods of democratic governments, elected leaders were no less callous in their disregard of constitutional governance or less brutal in attacking their political opponents. In fact, both military and the civilian governments exhibited a frightening degree of "garrison mentality"—that is, a mentality which promotes and/or supports the use of force or violence as the ultimate way to defeat or subdue political adversaries and to retain power. This culture of impunity has permeated—and been normalized in—different sectors of the Nigerian society. It has created an environment that has given rise to violent student fraternities in the country's tertiary institutions and, consequently, the development of garrison politics in the country.[3]

Since 1952, when the first student fraternity in Nigeria—the Pyrates Confraternity—came into existence, several splinter and new groups have emerged. According to Ekpo and Agbo (2005: 52–53), there are over eighty such student bodies across tertiary institutions in Nigeria. Many of these groups constitute serious security threats in the institutions where they operate. While there is little consensus on how student fraternities became violent, two schools of thought have emerged to explain the phenomenon. The first sees fraternity violence as resulting from the activities of the country's military intelligence agents in the 1980s and 1990s to destabilize the powerful national student organization, the National Association of Nigerian Students (NANS), and its campus affiliates. Those who subscribe to this view argue that long periods of military dictatorship in Nigeria—1966–79 and 1984–1999—made the emergence of a legal and potent political opposition difficult. With the suppression of democratic opposition, some civil society organizations (including the national student body) entered into alliances with one another, transforming themselves into a powerful underground opposition movement that coordinated sustained periods of disruptive antimilitary demonstrations. According to this perspective, the military intelligence took advantage of divisions among student fraternities to infiltrate these organizations and instigate conflicts among members, many of whom were political activists. To sustain this division, the military funded and armed competing groups in order to destabilize student solidarity and thus weaken NANS's ability to mobilize the student population for any form of antimilitary political action (*Economist* 2008; Eguavoen 2008; Ezeonu 2014).

The second school of thought associates fraternity violence with the schism that developed within such early groups as the Pyrates Confraternity, the Buccaneers, Black Axe, and the Supreme Vikings and the competition for dominance that followed the splitting up of these groups. This position is best articulated by Ekpo and Agbo (2005). These scholars point to the break of the Buccaneers from the Pyrates Confraternity at the University of Ibadan in the 1970s and the former's attempt to forcefully displace the latter as key to the emergence of fraternity violence in tertiary institutions (Ezeonu 2014).

While these two perspectives address the immediate causes of fraternity violence in Nigeria, they fail to account for the role of the country's enduring culture of violence and impunity. In fact, it is this national culture of violence that created the enabling environment for the militarization of student fraternities. For instance, the genocidal actions of the Nigerian state prior to and during the country's civil war in the late 1960s and early 1970s played out not only in the cities and villages of Northern and Western regions but also in tertiary institutions located in these regions. Several Igbo students and intellectuals residing outside their Eastern home region had to quickly return home to seek refuge for themselves and their families. Thus, while the first student fraternity in Nigeria started as an altruistic nonviolent student organization, this organization and the subsequent ones began in an environment in which a culture of violence was not only known but also defined access to power, prestige, and political influence.

It is common knowledge that during the country's long experience with military rule, civilian deference to members of the armed forces (usually elicited by brutal force or threats of it) was at its peak. Over time, this culture of deference to a garrisoned community—that is, an organized group that specializes on the use of violence, such as the military—soon became normalized. It is hardly surprising, therefore, that the use of violence as a mechanism to gain power and respect, and to exert influence, has been adopted by many student fraternities (see Ezeonu 2014). Although the violence associated with student fraternities used to be localized within the institutions where they operate, career politicians have increasingly found the groups useful in advancing their electoral objectives. Consequently, many of the fraternities have been incorporated into Nigeria's garrison politics, especially since the Fourth Republic. This has exacerbated the danger they pose to public security and democratic politics in Nigeria.

Methodology

This study took place at a university in the southern part of Nigeria. To protect the anonymity of my participants and to avoid any possibility of exposing them to harm, I have given the pseudonym, "University of the South,"[4] to this institution. This is a well-established practice in sociological studies (Whyte 1993; Marvasti 2004; Felde 2011). Data for this work was collected from August to December 2011 and involved a total of thirty participants, including faculty members, university administrators, and students.

Data was collected through ethnographic fieldwork, involving semistructured individual and focus-group interviews. Two focus-group interviews were used. The ethnographic fieldwork is a popular method of data collection in studies of this nature. The method particularly privileges the experiential knowledge of research subjects, which is shaped by their lived experience (Vigil 1988; Padilla 1992; Decker and Van Winkle 1996; Narag 2003; Venkatesh 2008).

Garrison Politics and the Co-optation of Student Fraternities

Harold Lasswell observes that in a classical garrison state, the recruitment of political leaders does not go through such democratic processes as periodic elections, "but by self-perpetuation through co-option" (Lasswell 1941: 462). However, contemporary scholars of garrison politics suggest that such states often have a facade of democracy, in which electoral choices are often rigged through the use of organized violence (Figueroa and Sives 2002; Clarke 2006). Nigeria is no exception. Beyond the well-documented co-option of the repressive state apparatus, members of student fraternities are engaged by desperate politicians as thugs and private armies to achieve parochial electoral objectives (Human Rights Watch 2007; Omotola 2007; Okolie 2010). Information from this study demonstrates that student fraternities are involved in the Nigerian garrison politics in two fundamental ways: political brigandage and group alumni associations.

Political Brigandage

Following the pattern in Jamaica where neighbourhood gangs have played an active role in the country's violent electoral politics, student fraternities have become the harbingers of electoral violence in Fourth Republic politics in Nigeria. Some of my respondents reported that

Nigerian politicians rely heavily on the fraternities for a steady supply of political thugs. Sixteen of these respondents identified this form of political association as a major source of funding for the fraternities. As in Jamaica, where politicians patronize neighborhood gangs for political ends (Figueroa and Sives 2002; Clarke 2006), politicians have become the major benefactors of student fraternities in Nigeria, using different forms of patronage to co-opt members of student fraternities to help them win and remain in power. Such patronage includes sponsoring fraternity events, funding their puppets in student union elections, helping fraternity leaders secure political party leadership positions, and sponsoring them in national elections. As one respondent pointed out,

> one of my former hostel mates who dropped out of school two years ago is already a local government chairman. This guy was a known rugged man while on campus. He knew every politician in town and was believed to be their point man for recruiting hard guys. The guy couldn't even graduate but is now the big man in [redacted] local government. This is Nigeria for you. And you're wondering why this country is so messed up. Those of us who are not in cults could hardly get jobs on graduation, but these hard guys don't even need to graduate to live well.[5]

This respondent went on to lament the symbiotic relationship between politicians and members of student fraternities, in which politicians depend on fraternity members to protect their electoral turfs and intimidate their opponents in exchange for all forms of political patronage.

Generally, politics is a big business in Nigeria. An electoral victory or a connection to people in powerful political positions produces enormous returns in terms of material wealth and political influence. Nigerian political office holders are probably among the highest paid in the world (Ejikeme 2012) and exert vast political influence with more offices enjoying immunity from prosecution than in many places in the world. For instance, while individuals holding the positions of the president, vice president, governor and deputy governor enjoy immunity from prosecution, other politically powerful people in the country are usually treated with deference by criminal justice officials, including the courts. Public accountability is hardly embedded in the national political culture, as the institutional framework to enforce it is weak or in some cases nonexistent. Many highly placed office holders, including state governors, federal and state legislators, and officials of ruling parties at the different levels of government, have been accused of stealing millions of dollars of public funds without any serious legal repercussion. This included the daughter of a former president, Olusegun Obasanjo, and a party chieftain closely connected to him. While the government's anticorruption agency, the Economic and Financial Crimes Commission (EFCC), tried to prosecute some of these individuals, those attempts were, in most cases, feeble and unserious as officials of the EFCC hold their offices at the pleasure of the president (EFCC 2011; Tell 2011). Critics have also accused the agency of being a tool in the hands of the president to persecute his political opponents (Inokoba and Ibegu 2011). Currently, the chairman of the Commission as well as the chairman of the country's Code of Conduct Tribunal are facing accusations of corruption (Daniel et al. 2015; Omoniyi 2015). Both individuals were appointed by the president. Given the weak institutional framework for the effective prosecution of the embezzlement of public funds, electoral politics has become both lucrative and attractive to a section of the country's politicians— hence the motivation for this category of politicians to win at all costs. It is this class of politicians that has established a relationship of convenience with a number of student fraternities to advance its political (and by extension, economic) agendas. Among the sixteen of my respondents who highlighted this sort of political alliance, a common assertion was that members of the fraternities were used as private armies of the politicians concerned, in most cases to intimidate, or where necessary, maim or assassinate political opponents. The fraternity members were also vital in perpetrating various forms of electoral fraud. With respect to the University of the South, the fraternities implicated in this type of alliance included the Pyrates Confraternity, the Black Axe, the Buccaneers, the Vikings, and the Eiye.

The general elections of April 2007 were probably the worst in the country since the democratic transition of 1999. From the local government elections to the presidential election, the exercise was characterized by widespread fraud, including deliberate delay of electoral materials, falsification of results, and the political intimidation of opponents. These fraudulent practices were perpetrated by both the politicians and the electoral officials themselves. The elections were marred by nationwide violence described by European Union monitors as among the worst that they had observed anywhere in the world (*Economist* 2007; Human Rights Watch 2007; Okolie 2010; Purefoy 2011).

Many respondents in this study reported that student fraternities played active roles in this electoral violence. In one focus-group discussion, respondents repeatedly highlighted the role of politicians in perpetuating and sustaining the violent activities of student fraternities, especially in the political arena. These respondents claimed that most of the sophisticated weapons used by fraternity groups were usually supplied by their political patrons, mostly for electoral violence. One respondent, "Marina,"[6] who dominated this focus-group discussion, reported that, during the 2007 presidential election, there was a close collaboration between members of student fraternities at the University of the South and officers of the Nigerian Police Force. He reported that on the day of the presidential election, some "known cultists" from the institution, who were living in private hostels close to the university, were taken by police vehicles to the ruling party headquarters in the state capital and that, after the election, many of these students returned with "wads of money." Marina, who was living in one of these hostels, stated that he was invited to join this expedition by one of his friends, whom he strongly believed to be a member of one of the violent fraternities on campus, but refused because of the inherent dangers involved.

Reporting on his discussions with this friend after the expedition,[7] Marina said that fraternity members recruited from the university worked with politicians to harass opponents and voters on Election Day at Onitsha, Awka and Nnewi (Anambra State), Benin City and Ekpoma (Edo State), and Abuja (the Federal Capital Territory). He stated that, in Abuja, these students were accommodated at the five-star Nicon Noga Hilton Hotel by one of the president's henchmen from Anambra State. According to him, this presidential aide has maintained an enduring relationship with fraternity leaders at the university over the years and has funded the election of some of them as leaders of the People's Democratic Party at the state level, as well as their involvement in the institution's students' union politics. The presidential aide was also said to have used these fraternity leaders to mobilize several "rent-a-crowd"[8] demonstrations in support of the former President Olusegun Obasanjo's failed bid to change the national constitution to enable him to serve a third presidential term. The activities evoke those of the enforcers of Jamaican garrison politics whose violence is nested within the partisan electoral strategies of the country's politicians. In line with this study, leaders of the violent groups which control Jamaica's garrison politics are valued by and incorporated into the leadership hierarchies of the political parties and are useful in mobilizing support for the parties' electoral success (Figueroa and Sives 2002).

The leadership of Nigeria's dominant political party, the People's Democratic Party (PDP), at the national, state, and local levels was particularly cited by most of the respondents for the increasing use of student fraternities to foment electoral violence. As one of these respondents who lost a cousin to such violence lamented,

the real criminals are those in the Presidency, the Governor's Office and the local government headquarters as well as the other desperate politicians especially in the PDP who are using these bad boys.

Holding the ruling party's hierarchy responsible for his cousin's death, the respondent said that her late cousin's fraternity co-opts members through a political aide of former President Olusegun Obasanjo to help facilitate election fraud that would help the federal ruling party win the 2007 presidential and gubernatorial elections in one of the southern states. Nevertheless, the groups that were involved in this fraud fell out over sharing of the money earmarked for this purpose and thus ended up in a serious intergroup clash that lasted for days. The respondent's cousin was killed in this conflict. Apparently because of the involvement of powerful politicians in the violent activities of these fraternities, law enforcement officials were generally reluctant to intervene. For instance, the respondent cited above reported that efforts by members of her extended family to get the police to investigate her cousin's murder and to prosecute the culprits proved futile as one of the officers investigating the case advised them to forget about the case as the incident was "a presidential matter." This apparently implied that the organization of the violence involved top politicians who were connected to the presidency. Commenting further on the co-option of violent student fraternities into the country's electoral politics, another respondent lamented that "unfortunately, most of the heavy weapons supplied by politicians are generally not returned after the election, so these guys are heavily armed and it is easy for them to terrorize the university community."

Nevertheless, the use of student fraternities to advance electoral objectives was not limited to the ruling party. Respondents mostly agreed that opposition politicians were also implicated. In fact, the involvement of different categories of politicians in this form of electoral violence has been well-documented (see Human Rights Watch 2007; Omotola 2007; Okolie 2010). A former member of the Supreme Eiye Confraternity, who claimed to have experienced a religious conversion and had therefore left the group, attested to his recruitment to work in the opposition stronghold of Ogun State. He said that he was among several members of his group recruited by politicians contesting elections under the platform of Action Congress (AC) to help the party to maintain control of its stronghold in this southwestern state.[9] He claimed that many of them were recruited from the University of the South, the University of Benin, the Auchi Polytechnic, and Obafemi Awolowo University. According to this respondent, whom I have given the pseudonym, "Heavyman" (because of his stout build), the AC believed that it would win Ogun State (which was the president's state of origin) in a free and fair election but was afraid that the President was desperate to manipulate the election after the humiliating defeat of his People's Democratic Party in the state in the 1999 presidential election. He explained that since the president's party was using the police and the military to intimidate opposition political parties, the Action Congress "got us involved as the [opposition] party's frontline soldiers to match the police and even the army and to guard the votes." Heavyman, who claimed to have worked for the Action Congress in this capacity for five years before the 2007 elections, said that, in the preceding presidential election (2003), he was in charge of the party's security both in Owan East and Owan West local government areas of Edo State. He was then a student at the Auchi Polytechnic. In other words, he had an enduring relationship with politicians as a member of the Supreme Eiye Confraternity.

The involvement of the opposition Action Congress in this violent electoral process was confirmed in an interview granted by its 2007 vice presidential candidate, Senator Ben Obi, to Human Rights Watch. In this interview, the senior opposition politician emphasized the political importance of violence in the electoral process and acknowledged employing the services of political thugs himself. According to him:

> Earlier I had 20 boys here to see me. If anyone tries to attack me my boys will unleash terror. . . . I help them to secure a little patronage from government or to start small businesses. . . . It is not possible to have a campaign without your boys (Human Rights Watch 2007: 28).

Another common opinion expressed in one of the focus-group discussions tied some of these student fraternities and their political patrons to the seemingly intractable problem of commercial kidnappings, especially in the southern states. As one of the participants pointed out:

> This is why cases of kidnapping go up especially during election years. Politicians engage cult guys to raise money for politics. Look at the calibre of people they go after; look at the type of money they demand for ransom. Where do they get the sophisticated weapons they use? You might think that I am a cult member by saying this. No, but this is common knowledge in this institution, and those in government cannot pretend not to be aware of this. That is why they are not serious about tackling the problem of kidnapping or cult violence.

This respondent was making reference to an upsurge in commercial kidnappings in Nigeria. While this form of organized crime started in the Niger Delta area of the country as part of a guerrilla strategy to oppose transnational petroleum-prospecting corporations in the region, since 2006 it has expanded to other parts of the country, especially the southeastern states. The motivation for this form of crime has also changed from sabotaging the economic activities of transnational corporations to creating a new form of trade in human commodities (Osumah and Aghedo 2011). Wealthy Nigerians and their relatives are particularly targeted and hefty ransoms, often running into millions of naira, are paid in exchange for the kidnapped victims. When ransom payments are delayed or not paid, or attempts are made to use security agents to rescue the kidnapped victims, such victims are sometimes murdered as a punishment for the recalcitrant family of the kidnapped. Victims of this form of organized crime have included wealthy businessmen, a former federal minister of finance who had also served as a secretary to the government of the federation, retired military officers, and a former deputy governor who was executed by his kidnappers reportedly over a disagreement involving ransom payments (Agborh 2013; Ekpu 2013; Lawal et al. 2015). With the disturbing rate of commercial kidnapping in southern Nigeria, the country has joined the other kidnapping hotspots (including Mexico, Colombia, and Ecuador) as one of the most dangerous places in the world to live. The Nigerian situation is particularly worrisome because of the alleged involvement of politicians in this criminal activity.[10]

The involvement of fraternity students in garrison politics in Nigeria is a sad reflection on both the poor quality of higher education in the country and the enduring national culture of violence. Prior to the incursion of the military into the country's political process, the Nigerian public education system was probably among the best in the world. The prejunta public education system produced some of the world's most celebrated scholars, including the legendary writer, Chinua Achebe; the Nobel laureate in literature, Wole Soyinka; the illustrious poet, Christopher Okigbo; the renowned mathematician, Chike Obi; distinguished historians Kenneth Dike and Ade Ajayi, among others. Nevertheless, public education has degenerated steadily since military rule in 1966. Constrained by years of government neglect, public education has virtually collapsed in contemporary Nigeria. This has exacerbated the growth and crisis of fraternity violence in tertiary institutions (for instance, see Ezeonu 2014).

In apparent reaction to the deterioration of public education in the country, wealthy parents are increasingly choosing to send their children abroad or to some of the country's exorbitant private universities. A few years ago, Sanusi Lamido Sanusi, the then governor of the Central Bank of Nigeria, estimated that about seventy-one thousand Nigerian students were studying in Ghanaian universities and that they paid around N155 billion (about $1 billion) in tuition fees (Ebije 2011). These figures were for Ghana alone, but very wealthy Nigerians prefer European and North American universities. Tuition in these places cost far more. So, the menace of student fraternities in Nigerian tertiary institutions goes beyond public-security challenges to impact the national economy directly.

No doubt, the participation of these fraternities in the nation's violent electoral process promises a turbulent future for the country. As Omotola observes, "garrisoned electoral processes [in Nigeria] represent a powerful source of democratic instability that can threaten the consolidation of democracy" (2009: 194). The same observation has been made of garrison politics in Jamaica (see Figueroa and Sives 2002).

Group Alumni Associations

Data from this study suggests that fellowships among members of student fraternities at the University of the South do not terminate upon graduation. Such fellowships continue after school and new graduate members sometimes depend on such old-boy networks to advance their professional careers and other interests. Whatever form these associations might take, respondents who promoted this position argued that fraternity members tend to advance their individual and collective goals upon graduation by maintaining postgraduate clusters of their groups after school. These respondents claimed that established fraternity alumni are known to help newer graduate members find employment in both the public and private sectors and to advance both professionally and materially. As the *Economist* put it in a report on Nigerian student fraternities,

> the pay-offs [of membership] after university can be no less rewarding. With a well-connected alumni network, students hope that their cult membership will win them a job in a country where most graduates are unemployed (2008).

A common observation among many respondents was that these fraternity alumni continue to organize fellowships under alternate names. For instance, alumni members of the Pyrates Confraternity were reported to organize themselves as the National Association of Seadogs; ex-members of the Supreme Vikings Confraternity operate as the De Norsemen Klub of Nigeria or sometimes the National Association of Adventurers; former members of the Supreme Eiye Confraternity operate as the National Association of Airlords; while former members of Black Axe operate as the Neo-Black Movement of Africa. Heavyman, the respondent mentioned earlier, pointed out that such alumni networks even had branches abroad, including Britain, the United States, and Canada. He claimed that the National Association of Seadogs had branches in the Canadian provinces of Ontario and Alberta; the states of Georgia, California, New York, and Texas; and many cities in the United Kingdom. According to him, while De Norsemen Klub of Nigeria had a presence in the United Kingdom and Germany, it was particularly active in North America, especially in Texas, which has a large population of Nigerians.

Some of my respondents believe that the use of these alternative names help the fraternity alumni members to deal with the credibility problem associated with the notorious and criminal activities of campus-based groups. For instance, in a disclaimer placed in the Nigerian national newspaper, *The Guardian*, on October 18, 2011, the Pyrates Confraternity vigorously defended its organizational credibility in the face of the persistent association of the group with campus-based fraternity groups that operate under the same name. Emphasizing the termination of its campus branches since 1984, the confraternity denounced student groups which were still misrepresenting themselves as its campus branches and threatened legal action against such groups if they continued such misrepresentations (*The Guardian* 2011; Ezeonu 2014). Nevertheless, when I pointed out this disclaimer in the two focus-group discussions organized in this study, many respondents strongly questioned the claim that the external organization was structurally different from the campus-based ones. They pointed out that the campus-based groups also use the same alternate names popularly adopted by the alumni groups, a claim supported by Ekpo and Agbo (2005).

However, one important area of postgraduation alliance commonly identified by many respondents in this study is the political sphere. A majority of my respondents (70%) believed that fraternity alumni either belong to the same political groups or collaborate with one another in the pursuit of their political aspirations. They claimed that these alumni clusters actively organize alliances to capture state power at different levels of government. Data from this study indicate that this was at least the case for the major fraternities at the University of the South. As one academic staff member to whom I gave the pseudonym, "Dr. Quest," put it,

> It is unbelievable, but many of the present cohort of political leaders in Nigeria, from the local government to the highest office in the land, were former cultists who terrorized our tertiary institutions as students. They are now extending the same level of terror to the rest of the nation. Many of these guys are violent criminals, for lack of a better word. And now, just look at what they have turned the country into.

Several respondents mentioned the names of some famous politicians, including federal and state legislators, whom they alleged to have been members of fraternities as students of the University of the South. For legal reasons, I have avoided including the names of these politicians in this article. A former executive member of the institution's student union government who participated in this study believed that about a third of the elected members of the legislature of the state in which the university is located were either current or former fraternity members. He added that,

> a serving governor of one of the [southern] states is a known frat member and associates openly with one of these groups. Ask any student in this institution; most students know about this. In fact, joining or fraternizing with one of these dangerous fraternities is one avenue to achieve political success in this country. That's Nigerian democracy for you.

Evidently, these claims are not without merit. According to *The Economist* (2008), "alumni of the Vikings Confraternity, for example, claim at least 11 members of the Rivers State House of Assembly."[11] Omoruyi (2014: 1) expresses a similar sentiment when he argues that in Nigeria, the effect of student fraternities "has moved from who controls the campus to who controls the state houses of assembly, House of Representatives, senators, governors and other public offices." While student fraternities in Nigeria are clearly not the only such groups known to invest in the capture and use of state power (Sutton 2002; Sora 2003; Brown 2013; Mallari 2014), the violence of their approach represents a potential threat to the development of an enduring democratic political culture in Nigeria.

Across time and political space, fraternities have been known to wield enormous power in the political process of many countries, including the democratic ones. One fraternity commonly associated in popular discourse with having a grip on political power in the United States is the Order of the Skull and Bones. This fraternity was established in 1832 at Yale University as Chapter 322 of a German secret society and has a reputation for extending an enormous political and economic network to its members upon graduation. It is believed that this network significantly aids and/or consolidates their upward social mobility in the United States. Studies document that, despite the fact that only fifteen students are accepted into this exclusive student fraternity annually, its alumni include at least three former US presidents: William Howard Taft, George H. W. Bush, and George W. Bush; many congressmen, elite military officers, judges (including a former justice of the Supreme Court, Potter Stewart), the current secretary of state, John Kerry; the founder of *Time* magazine, Henry Luce; "and an assortment of CIA officials, Fortune 500 CEOs, and politicians who . . . have had the president's proverbial ear" (Brown 2013: 1; see also Sutton 2002; Sora 2003). According to Anthony Sutton, who claimed to have had the privilege of seeing the membership list once, "glancing through the sheets it was more than obvious—this was no ordinary group. The names spelled Power, with a capital P" (Sutton 2002: 9).

The 2004 presidential election in the United States is believed to have been fought by two identified members of this organization, President George W. Bush of the Republican Party and Senator John Kerry of the Democratic Party. In two separate interviews granted to the late American television journalist, Tim Russert of the National Broadcasting Company (NBC), neither candidate denied membership of this fraternity. Refusing to discuss his involvement with this organization, President G. W. Bush told Russert that the organization was "so secret we can't talk about it" (see National Broadcasting Corporation 2004a). Similarly, Senator Kerry said that there was "not much" to talk about since "it's a secret" (see National Broadcasting Corporation 2004b). While both candidates laughed off Russert's question regarding their memberships, they refused to deny it. In fact, the membership of this organization included some of the most powerful men in the United States, who have shaped and continue to shape world politics (Leung 2003).

In the Philippines, alumni of student fraternities are known to mobilize electoral support for their members. The country's current vice president and presidential candidate in the 2016 election, Jejomar Binay, is reported to have been a beneficiary of such support. Known to have been a member of the Alpha Phi Omega (APO) fraternity since his student days at the University of the Philippines Dilima in the 1960s, Binay was reported to have credited the support of this fraternity for his 2010 Vice Presidential election victory. He has also benefitted from its support while fighting off an allegation of political corruption (see Mallari 2014). The Alpha Phi Omega fraternity is still active at Filipino universities today and is among fraternities that use violence to foster brotherhood (Sison 2015).

As has been demonstrated, the capture of the different levers of national politics by members or affiliates of fraternities is not peculiar to Nigeria.

Nevertheless, given the infancy of Nigerian democracy, the emergence and potential domination of national politics by members and alumni of student fraternities have worrying implications for the development of a democratic culture in the country. In fact, three potential implications immediately come to mind. First, after many years of military dictatorship, there is a danger of violent groups recapturing the apparatuses of the state, thus creating a pseudodemocracy managed and controlled by belligerent patricians. In the consequent organized oligarchic rule, the consent of the people as the basis of the legitimacy of governments would become inconsequential. As demonstrated in many states of the federation (Omoruyi 2004; Human Rights Watch 2007; Economist 2008), the gestation of garrison politics in Nigeria would leave political power in the hands of individuals who in more functional societies would be in prison, rather than in public office.

Secondly, a mature liberal democracy (devoid of possible capture by organized violent groups with parochial interests) is critical to eliminating the national culture of impunity that has festered in Nigeria following many years of military dictatorships. For instance, the concept of the "bloody civilians" used informally by members of the armed forces, during military regimes, to demonstrate the powerlessness and subservience of the civilian population has continued in different forms under democratization. Politicians and senior officials of government still treat Nigerians with utter contempt, especially with respect to the constitutional and material entitlements of citizenship as well as in the social character of class relations. One example of this contempt was the November 2013 encounter between the Governor of Edo State, Adam Oshiomole, and a poor widow in the state capital, Benin City. Clearly enraged by the widow's alleged violation of a state law that regulates street trading, Oshiomole ordered the confiscation of the woman's wares. When the woman pleaded for mercy, informing the governor of her poor status as a sole-income widow, the governor became infuriated even further and, while insulting the poor widow, pointedly told her, "Go and Die" (see Oke 2013). Subsequently, in reaction to public opinion on this incident, Oshiomole apologized to the widow and tried to pacify public opinion by offering her a menial job with the government. This particular incident typified the arrogance, aggression, and impunity of the Nigerian political class, which is an imperious residual of the military era. Oshiomole's behavior was particularly shocking because he had built his political career on an antimilitary and antiauthoritarian activism as a national labour leader. That he would behave like the same military dictators that he criticized in the past demonstrates the nature of the culture of violence in which Nigerian democracy is nested.

Thirdly, the consolidation of garrison politics controlled by the alumni of violent fraternities in Nigeria will potentially provide the surest route to the political balkanization of the country's neighbourhoods and communities. The gang-controlled garrison communities in Jamaica provide good examples of this danger (see Figueroa and Sives 2002; Clarke 2006). Such a partisan segregation of neighbourhoods has become a common feature of Jamaican garrison politics, where certain urban neighbourhoods are controlled by party-affiliated gangs or nongovernmental armed groups. For example, in the 1970s, two partisan violent gangs (the Shower Posse and the Spanglers) operated as the unofficial private armies of that country's two leading political parties—the Jamaican Labour Party and the People's National Party. They controlled different neighbourhoods, and over time, garrison communities became an enduring feature of the country's democratic experience (Clarke 2006). While periodic elections continue to take place in Jamaica, there is no doubt that the citizens' freedom to choose the leadership of the country, especially within the garrison communities, has been compromised by intimidation and fear.

Groups colloquially defined as gangs (including criminal and/or political ones) are known to be territorial, and the aspiration to control particular territories exclusively for their activities is one defining characteristic of these groups. Despite the negative impact of ethnic politics in Nigeria, citizens still associate freely across neighbourhoods, cities, ethnic and regional lines. Nevertheless, the capture of state power by members and alumni of student fraternities may lead to the balkanization of the country's neighbourhoods and communities along parochial political lines. While the possible residential segregation of supporters may serve the short-term interests of the politicians who fund and use these groups, the segregated neighbourhoods may eventually be taken over by criminal mobs or dons and thus pose significant public-security challenges in the long term. Given the chaotic and unsteady nature of Nigerian democracy, the greater involvement of organized violent groups such as student fraternities will worsen an already bad situation.

Conclusion

Research on public-security challenges in Nigeria sometimes focuses, almost exclusively, on the activities of organized criminal groups that use lethal violence to achieve their parochial objectives. While many of these groups no doubt pose potent and enduring threats to public security in Nigeria, the current security discourse in the country nonetheless is deficient in its neglect of the equally threatening and disabling political praxis involving student fraternities, their alumni and political collaborators. Using a modified construct of garrison politics, this article examines the gestation of these violent groups in the politics of Nigeria's Fourth Republic as well as the real and potential implications of their capture of state power.

Employing individual and focus-group interviews from members of a southern tertiary institution to which I have given the pseudonym, the University of the South, I have highlighted the entrenched relationship between some of the country's politicians and members of student fraternities as well as the emergence of the alumni of these fraternities as powerful and fearsome contenders and wielders of state power in the politics of the Fourth Republic. Given the intractable electoral violence in Nigeria, members and alumni of these fraternities and their political collaborators are likely to shape the future political landscape of the country, albeit with ominous political consequences.

Notes

1. Since its independence from British colonial rule in 1960, Nigeria has had only four periods of democratic rule. All of these democratic experiments were interrupted by periods of military rule. The periods of democratic rule are as follows: 1963–66 (First Republic), 1979–83 (Second Republic), 1991–1993 (Third Republic), and 1999–date (Fourth Republic).
2. I choose to describe kidnapping for ransom in this way because, in its present form in Nigeria, it is undertaken purely for economic gain.
3. A similar observation has been made in respect of a related effect of "militarisation of Filipino society" on the militarization of student fraternities in that country—specifically during the period of martial law under Ferdinand Marcos (Narag 2003: 12).
4. I am grateful to Professor BikoAgozino of Virginia Tech for very helpful suggestions in this regard.
5. Fraternities are often known colloquially as "cults" in most tertiary institutions in Nigeria. Fraternity members in this particular institution generally refer to themselves as "rugged men," "hard guys," or "happening guys" and to nonmembers as "bloody civilians." The last argot was apparently influenced by several years of military dictatorship in Nigeria, a period during which the members of the armed forces brutalized the civilian population whom they commonly referred to as "bloody civilians." For security and legal reasons, I have deliberately withheld the name of the local government area where this individual was alleged to be the political head. A local government area is the third level of Nigeria's federal arrangement. The other two are the federal and state governments. Note that the phrase "big man" is a Nigerian pidginEnglish expression for an important person or a boss.
6. This is a pseudonym used to identify one of the most active participants in the focus-group interviews.
7. With the precise nature of the information provided by Marina, I suspected that he was a member of one of the fraternities himself and had probably participated

in the activities he discussed. However, ethical considerations prevented me from questioning him about this, first, because it would be improper to raise probing questions about these issues in a focus-group context, and, second, prior to the interview I had instructed them not to tell me if they were members of a fraternity or had participated in violence or any form of crime associated with fraternities or knew anyone who had. I explained to them that if they informed me about any crime in which they were involved, I might be required by law to notify the police.

8. This is a practice in Nigeria where politicians and interest groups sometimes offer money to people (mostly youth) to participate in demonstrations in support of or against (mostly government) policies or decisions. The demonstrators are often not interested in the issue concerned but are motivated to demonstrate by the promise of a monetary reward.

9. The Action Congress was in opposition at the federal level but was in power in most of the southwestern states.

10. For a good discussion of this form of organized crime, see Osumah and Aghedo (2011).

11. The university where this study took place is not located in Rivers State. Rather, this quotation is used to support the data on the increasing influence of student fraternities in the Nigerian political process.

References

Achebe, Chinua. 2012. *There Was a Country: A Personal History of Biafra*. New York: Penguin Press.

Agborh, Alphonsus. 2013. "Retired Army Officer, Wife Kidnapped."*Nigerian Tribune*. (December 2). Retrieved March 27, 2014 (http://www.tribune.com.ng/news2013/index.php/en/news/newsheadlines/item/27655-retired-army-officer,-wife-kidnapped.html).

Aron, Raymond. 1979. "Remarks on Lasswell's 'The Garrison State'." *Armed Forces and Society* 5(3):347–359.

Bird, S. Elizabeth and Fraser Ottanelli. 2011. "The History and Legacy of the Asaba, Nigeria, Massacres."*African Studies Review* 54(3):1–26.

Brown, Buster. 2013. "Skull and Bones: It's Not Just for White Dudes Anymore." *The Atlantic*. (February 25). Retrieved January 15, 2014 (http://www.theatlantic.com/national/archive/2013/02/skull-and-bones-its-not-just-for-white-dudes-anymore/273463/).

Clarke, Colin. 2006. "Politics, Violence and Drugs in Kingston, Jamaica."*Bulletin of Latin American Research* 25(3):420–440.

Community Leadership Initiative. 2011. "The Birth of Nigerian Campus Cult/Gang Groups and its Consequences." Retrieved January 17, 2013 (http://www.campuscults.net/index.html).

Constitution of the Federal Republic of Nigeria. 1999. "Section 308: Restrictions on Legal Proceedings."

Dains, Ronald N. 2004. *Lasswell's Garrison State Reconsidered: Exploring a Paradigm Shift in U.S. Civil-Military Relations Research*. Unpublished PhD. Dissertation. Tuscaloosa, AL: University of Alabama.

Daniel, Soni et al. 2015. "Alleged Unremitted N2.05trn: Senate in Disarray Over EFCC Probe."*Vanguard* (August 27). Retrieved October 17, 2015 (http://www.vanguardngr.com/2015/08/alleged-unremitted-n2-05ltrn-senate-in-disarray-over-efcc-probe/).

Decker, Scott H. and Barrick Van Winkle. 1996. *Life in the Gang: Family, Friends, and Violence*. New York: Cambridge University Press.

Dudley, Billy. 1965. "Violence in Nigerian Politics." *Transition* 5(21):21–24.

Ebije, Noah. 2011. "Nigeria's Political Structure Wasteful - CBN Gov." *Daily Sun.* (October 30). Retrieved November 11, 2013 (http://sunnewsonline.com/webpages/news/national/2011/oct/30/national-30-10-2011-005.html).

EFCC. 2011. "Economic & Financial Crime Commission, EFCC: On-Going High Profile Cases – 2007–2010." Retrieved December 30, 2011 (http://www.efccnigeria.org/jm15/index.php/information-center/high-profile-cases).

Eguavoen, Irit. 2008. "Killer Cults on Campus. Secrets, Security and Services Among Nigerian Students." *Sociologus* 1:1–25.

Ejikeme, Anene. 2012. "Nigerian Anger Boils Over." *The New York Times* (January 12). Retrieved May 22, 2013 (http://www.nytimes.com/2012/01/13/opinion/nigerian-anger-boils-over.html?_r=0).

Ekpo, Akpan H. and Anayochukwu Agbo. 2005. *Behind the Mask: The Untold Secrets of Secret Cults in Nigeria.* Port Harcourt, Nigeria: Wordcraft Books.

Ekpu, Dom. 2013. "I Offered Kidnappers N1bn Ransom - GU Motors Boss." *The Sun.* (November 12). Retrieved November 20, 2013 (http://sunnewsonline.com/new/national/offered-kidnappers-n1bn-ransom-gu-motors-boss/).

Ekwe-Ekwe, Herbert. 2006. *Biafra Revisited.* Dakar and Reading, MA: African Renaissance.

Ekwe-Ekwe, Herbert. 2011. *Readings from Reading: Essays on African Politics, Genocide, Literature.* Dakar and Reading, MA: African Renaissance.

Ezeonu, Ifeanyi. 2014. "Violent Fraternities and Public Security Challenges in Nigerian Universities: A Study of the 'University of the South.'" *Journal of African American Studies* 18(3):269–285.

Falola, Toyin. 2009. *Colonialism and Violence in Nigeria.* Bloomington, IN: Indiana University Press.

Felde, Lina Hoel. 2011. "Elevated Cholesterol as Biographical Work - Expanding the Concept of 'Biographical Disruption'." *Qualitative Sociology Review* 7(2):101–120.

Figueroa, Mark and Amanda Sives. 2002. "Homogenous Voting, Electoral Manipulation and the 'Garrison' Process in Post-Independence Jamaica." *Commonwealth and Comparative Politics* 40(1):81–108.

Fitch, J. Samuel. 1985. "The Garrison State in America: A Content Analysis of Trends in the Expectation of Violence." *Journal of Peace Research* 22(1):31–45.

Florquin, Nicolas and Eric G. Berman, eds. 2005. *Armed and Aimless: Armed Groups, Guns, and Human Security in the Ecowas Region.* Geneva: Small Arms Survey, Graduate Institute of International Affairs, Geneva.

Friedberg, Aaron L. 1992. "Why Didn't the United States Become a Garrison State?" *International Security* 16(4):109–142.

Human Rights Watch. 2007. *Criminal Politics: Violence, "Godfathers" and Corruption in Nigeria.* (Research Report). Vol.19 (16A). October: 1–121.

Inokoba, Preye K. and Weleayam T. Ibegu. 2011. "Economic and Financial Crime Commission (EFCC) and Political Corruption: Implication for the Consolidation of Democracy in Nigeria." *Anthropologist* 13(4):283–291.

Kemedi, Dimieari Von. 2006. "Fuelling the Violence: Non-State Armed Actors (Militia, Cults, and Gangs) in the Niger Delta." *Niger Delta: Economies of Violence* (Working Paper No. 10). Institute of International Studies, University of California, Berkeley/The United States Institute of Peace, Washington DC/Our Niger Delta, Port Harcourt, Nigeria.

Lasswell, Harold D. 1941. "The Garrison State."*American Journal of Sociology* 46(4):455–468.

Lawal, Iyabo et al. 2015." Olu Falae Kidnapped on his 77th Birthday: Abductors Demand 100 million." *The Guardian* (Nigeria). (September 22). Retrieved October 15, 2015 (http://www.ngrguardiannews.com/2015/09/olu-falae-kidnapped-on-his-77th-irthday/).

Leslie, Glaister. 2010. *Confronting the Don: The Political Economy of Gang Violence in Jamaica.* Geneva: Small Arms Survey, Graduate Institute of International Affairs, Geneva.

Leung, Rebecca. 2003. "Secret Yale Society Includes America's Power Elite."*CBS.* (October 2). Retrieved December 25, 2013 (http://www.cbsnews.com/news/skull-and-bones/).

Levy, Horace. 2009. Inner City Killing Street: Reviving Community. Kingston, Jamaica: Arawak Monograph Series.

Mallari, Delfin T. 2014. "APO mobilizes 100,000 members to support 'Brod Jojo'". *Inquirer Southern Luzon* (October 25). Retrieved October 10, 2015 (http://newsinfo.inquirer.net/646913/apo-mobilizes-100000-members-to-support-brod-jojo).

Marvasti, Amir B. 2004. *Qualitative Research in Sociology.* London: Sage Publications.

Matusitz, Jonathan and Michael Repass. 2009. "Gangs in Nigeria: An Updated Examination." *Crime, Law and Social Change* 52(5):495–511.

Narag, Raymund. 2003. "Fraternity Violence and Small Arms: Impacts on Student Security in Five Manila Universities." p.12 in Robert Muggah and Yeshua Puangsuwan, eds. *Whose Security Counts? Participatory Research on Armed Violence and Human Insecurity in Southeast Asia.* Geneva: Small Arms Survey.

National Broadcasting Corporation. 2004a. "Transcript for Feb. 8th [Meet the Press]. Guest: President George W. Bush." Retrieved February 3, 2014 (http://www.nbcnews.com/id/4179618/ns/meet_the_press/t/transcript-feb-th/#.UvFXUNGA3IU).

National Broadcasting Corporation. 2004b. "Transcript for April 18 [Meet the Press]. Guest: Sen. John Kerry, D-MA, Presidential Candidate." Retrieved February 3, 2014. (http://www.nbcnews.com/id/4772030/ns/meet_the_press/t/transcript-april/#.UvFY6dGA3IU).

Nyiayaana, Kialee. 2011. "From University Campuses to Villages: A Study of Grassroots-based Cult Violence in Ogoniland."*ERAS* 12(2). (March). Retrieved January 4, 2011 (http://arts.monash.edu.au/publications/eras/edition-12-issue-2/articles/knyiayaana.pdf).

Oke, Ikeogu. 2013. "Governor Oshiomhole and the widow of Edo."*Punch.* (December 13). Retrieved February 13, 2014 (http://www.punchng.com/opinion/governor-oshiomhole-and-the-widow-of-edo/).

Okolie, Andrew. 2010. "The 2007 General Elections in Nigeria: An Account of the Politics of Personal Rule in an African Country by a former Presidential Aide." *Review of Black Political Economy* 37(2):153–172.

Omoniyi, Tosin. 2015. "Investigations: Code of Conduct Tribunal Chairman Battles Corruption Allegations." *Premium Times.* (July 14). Retrieved October 17, 2015 (http://www.premiumtimesng.com/investigationspecial-reports/186645-investigation-code-of-conduct-tribunal-chairman-battles-corruption-allegations.html).

Omotola, J. Shola. 2009. "'Garrison' Democracy in Nigeria: The 2007 General Elections and the Prospects of Democratic Consolidation." *Commonwealth and Comparative Politics* 47(2):194–220.

Omoruyi, Paul. 2014. "Life of Nigerian Cultists in America." *Saturday Newswatch.* (February 8). Retrieved February 8, 2014 (http://www.mydailynewswatchng.com/2014/02/08/life-nigerian-cultists-america/).

Osumah, Oarhe and Iro Aghedo. 2011. "Who Wants to be a Millionaire? Nigerian Youths and the Commodification of Kidnapping." *Review of African Political Economy* 38(128):277–287.

Padilla, Felix. 1992. *The Gang as an American Enterprise.* New Brunswick, NJ: Rutgers University Press.

Purefoy, Christian. 2011. "Violence Marks Run-up to Nigerian Elections".*CNN*. (March 31). Retrieved May 25, 2013 (http://www.cnn.com/2011/WORLD/africa/03/31/nigeria.elections/index.html).

Rotimi, Adewale. 2005. "Violence in the Citadel: The Menace of Secret Cults in the Nigerian Universities." *Nordic Journal of African Studies* 14(1):79–98.

Sison, Jose C. 2015. "Culture of Violence." The Philippine Star. (September 2). Retrieved October 15, 2015 (http://www.philstar.com/opinion/2015/09/02/1494936/culture-violence).

Sives, Amanda. 2002. "Changing Patrons, From Politician to Drug Don: Clientelism in Downtown Kingston, Jamaica." *Latin American Perspectives* 126(5):66–89.

Sora, Steven. 2003. *Secret Societies of America's Elites: From the Knights Templar to Skull and Bones*. Rochetser, VT: Destiny Books.

Stanley, Jay. 1996. "Harold Lasswell and the Idea of the Garrison State." *Society* 33(6):46–52.

Sutton, Anthony C. 2002. *America's Secret Establishment: An Introduction to the Order of Skull and Bones*. Walterville, OR: Trine Day.

Tell. 2011. "House Speaker Dimeji Bankole Arrested by EFCC." Retrieved December 30, 2011 (http://www.tellng.com/index.php?option=com_k2&view=item&id=315:house-speaker-dimeji-bankole-arrested-by-efcc).

The Economist. 2007. "Big Men, Big Fraud and Big Trouble." (April 26). Retrieved May 25, 2013 (http://www.economist.com/node/9070922).

The Economist. 2008. "Cults of Violence: How Student Fraternities Turned into Powerful and Well-Armed Gangs." (July 31). Retrieved October 15, 2015 (http://www.economist.com/node/11849078).

The Guardian. 2011. "National Association of Seadogs/Pyrates Confraternity: Disclaimer." October 19.

Tse-Tung, Mao. 1969. *Selected Works of Mao Tse-Tung. Vol.II*. Peking: Foreign Languages Press.

Venkatesh, Sudhir. 2008. *Gang Leader for a Day: A Rogue Sociologist Takes to the Street*. New York: Penguin Press.

Vigil, James D. 1988. *Barrio Gangs: Street Life and Identity in Southern California*. Austin, TX: University of Texas Press.

Whyte, William Foote. 1993. *Street Corner Society: The Social Structure of an Italian Slum. 4th ed*. Chicago: University of Chicago Press.

Defining Success in the Military Advising Mission[1]

Remi M. Hajjar
United States Military Academy

Political and Military Sociology: An Annual Review, 2016, Vol. 44: 51–78.

This research examines how military advisors define success in their unconventional, ambiguous mission. This project's data stem from multimethod research, including data collected in Iraq, documents, and interviews. The article presents findings that reveal an intriguing story about how advisors conceive advisory success. It discusses the core patterns of "Iraqi (or any counterpart) Good Enough," advisors working themselves out of a job, and constructing enduring relationships. I argue that effective advisors deploy a multifaceted Swiss Army knife of cultural tools, including peacekeeper-diplomat, warrior, subject matter expert, innovator, and others, which reveal broader changes indicative of emergent postmodern military culture.

Introduction

Since 9/11, millions of US and coalition military service members have been deployed to Iraq and Afghanistan, and tens of thousands have served as military advisors to foreign security forces. In the military advising mission, advisors provide foreign counterparts (CP) (security forces) consultation, professional advice, recommendations, and access to US logistics, enablers (e.g., medical services, intelligence, etc.), and effects (such as artillery and air strikes). One conundrum inherent in conducting this important contemporary mission constitutes how to conceive or measure success. This article draws on data from a study of the US military advising mission to report findings about how advisors define success. It contributes to postmodern military theory (Moskos, Williams, and Segal 2000; Williams 2008) through a discussion of postmodern military culture (Hajjar 2014a). It defines the military advising mission, forwards a theoretical framework, explains the method, discusses the major findings about defining advisory success, explicates implications, and concludes with ideas for future research.

What is the Military Advising Mission?

The essence of the advising mission constitutes military members providing training, advice, mentorship, coaching, and other related activities to foreign counterparts to enhance their capabilities and professionalism. Advising missions range from large-scale operations during combat conditions, such as in Iraq and Afghanistan after 9/11, to much smaller peacetime advisory efforts in numerous locations worldwide. Although advising is not a new role for the US military (particularly for the US Army Special Forces) (Ramsey 2006; Stoker 2008), the employment of many thousands of mainstream advisors in Iraq and Afghanistan represents a monumental adaptation in the conventional armed forces.

Figure 1[4]
The Military Advising Triad: One Example of an Advising Relationship

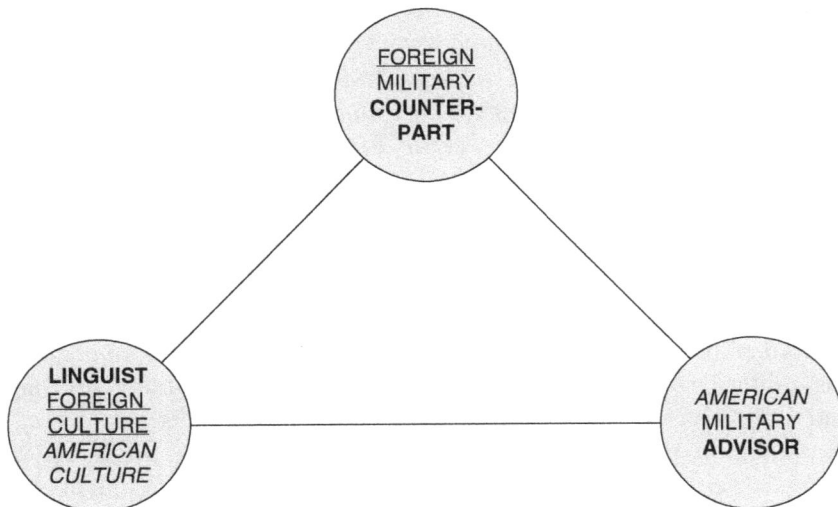

FOREIGN
MILITARY
**COUNTER-
PART**

LINGUIST
FOREIGN
CULTURE
AMERICAN
CULTURE

AMERICAN
MILITARY
ADVISOR

Three Classic Actors in a Military Advising Relationship

Bold = Actor's Role	*Italics = American Culture*
<u>Underline = Counterpart's Culture</u>	Normal Lettering = Military Culture

Advising relationships can take the form of different kinds of structures, but at their core they involve three principal actors (see figure 1). The first actor entails the foreign security force member in the advising relationship who bears the title of counterpart. Counterparts receive training, suggestions, tutelage, information, and associated support from the advisor. The second actor is the military advisor[2] who provides the counterpart with tutorship, teaching, advice, recommendations, and other forms of assistance intended to develop the counterpart's competence and performance. A third actor[3] plays a vital yet sometimes subdued role in the advising relationship, and this person bears the title of linguist. The linguist, employed by the US military, possesses sufficient cross-cultural competence (Hajjar 2010) and language skills (e.g., English and the counterpart's language) to facilitate effective communication and relationship building between the advisor and counterpart. In sum, in the advising relationship the advisor works with a linguist to provide assistance, suggestions, and consultation to increase the counterpart's proficiency and professionalism.

Literature Review: Building an Overarching Framework for Postmodern Military Culture

The first major relevant literature for this project constitutes the post-modern military theory (Moskos, Williams, and Segal 2000; Williams 2008). The postmodern military theory explores a dozen salient variables that help to explain the relationship between western armed forces and their societies. The theory describes the armed forces' evolution across four different eras from 1900 to the present in which each period ushers in increased sophistication based on new missions, threats, service members, and other factors. Although the model indirectly discusses culture and associated developments, it problematically lacks a culture variable. A recent report establishes the necessity of including a new culture variable in the postmodern military theory and advances a postmodern military culture framework (Harvey 1989; Zalmon 2006/2007; Winslow 2007; Williams 2008; Hajjar 2014a) (see figure 2). This framework reveals that contemporary military culture possesses tremendous complexity, frag-mentation, contradiction and harmony, traditional and current features, and multiple overlapping spheres of influence, including professional and bureaucratic (Ritzer 1975; Segal and Segal 1983; Abbott 1988; Hajjar and Ender 2005; Wong 2005), institutional (Janowitz 1977; Moskos and Wood 1988; Siebold 2001; Kelty 2008; Kelty and Bierman 2013) and

Figure 2
Postmodern Military Culture

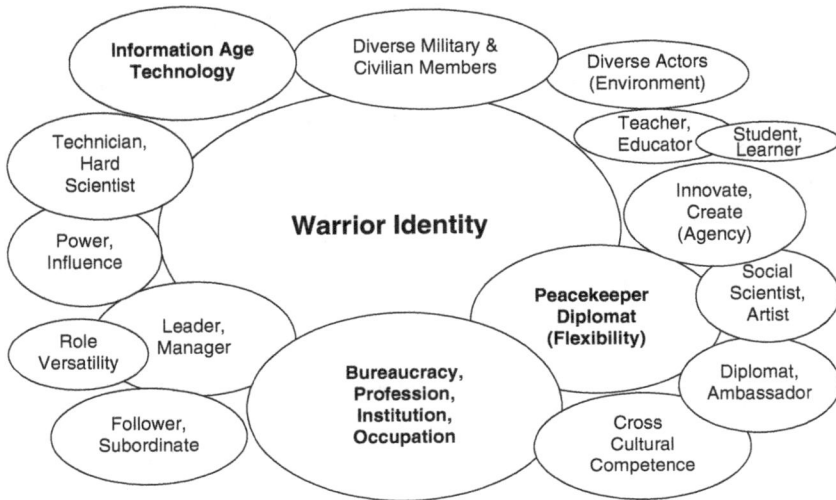

occupational, warrior, peacekeeper-diplomat, leadership and followership, multirole (Turner 1988; Montgomery 1998; Miles 2012) versatility, cross-cultural competence, power (French and Raven 1960; Etzioni 1961) and influence (Yukl and Tracey 1992), diplomacy (Perez 2012), ambassadorship, and other cultural spheres. This postmodern military culture theory serves as the overarching framework applied in this article, and the following discussions illuminate specific cultural spheres within this model.

This project deploys a flexible, pragmatic, and advantageous cultural toolkit (Swidler 1986, 2001) theory that differs from more traditional and unified views of culture (Geertz 1973; Griswold 1994; Schein 2010) that do not adequately account for culture's ambiguities, fragmentations, and conflicts. This supple toolkit provides a more complete comprehension of contemporary military culture. This article defines culture (Swidler 1986, 2001; Sewell 1992; Griswold 1994; DiMaggio 1997; Winslow 2007; Ender 2009) as a contested toolkit filled with orientations, tools, schemas (cognitive structures), frames, codes, narratives, habits, styles, language, symbols, values, beliefs, and assumptions that provide a group, organization, or society with shared meaning, a collective identity, and strategies of action. This definition applies Swidler's cultural toolkit, which malleably allows the existence of oppositional cultural tools, such as interdependence and autonomy in intimate relationships

(Swidler 2001, 1986). This conception of culture also utilizes Winslow's suitable military culture theory that includes integration, differentiation, and fragmentation; in particular, the fragmented nature of contemporary wars and armed forces supports the rise of postmodern military culture (Winslow 2006; Zalmon 2007).

Another fundamental theoretical underpinning of the postmodern military culture framework applied in this article involves the warrior–peacekeeper-diplomat paradigm (Williams 2008; Perez 2012; Hajjar 2014a) (see figure 3). The warrior–peacekeeper-diplomat model shows a historical comparison of traditional warrior-centric military culture and emergent postmodern military culture that also includes nascent peacekeeper-diplomat cultural orientations and tools. The traditional warrior identity (see left column of figure 3) consists of command, combat, conformist, and ethnocentric orientations. Patton serves as the modern era prototype of a hard-charging commander who effectively accomplished combat missions but who is not well-known for cultural savviness or diplomacy. Petreaus serves as the archetype for the postmodern era because he was a well-known tough combat leader (indicative of some warrior qualities) while simultaneously drawing on sophisticated cross-cultural and political

Figure 3
Comparison of Two Major U.S. Military Cultural Orientations and Sets of Tools:
Warrior and Peacekeeper-Diplomat

Era	20th Century Modern Culture (1900 –1990)	Emergent Postmodern Culture (1990 –Present) (New Cultural Toolkit)
Major Identity (Role)	Warrior Identity	Peacekeeper-Diplomat Role, Warrior Identity (& Other Cultural Orientations)
Associated Cultural Orientations and Tools	**Command Orientations:** - Actively Direct, Order, Impose, Tell, Demand, Take Charge **Traditional Combat Orientations:** - Break, Destroy, Kill, Capture, Incapacitate, Dominate - Dehumanize: Systematic "Othering" Process Facilitates Insensitivity and Fighting **Conformist Orientations:** - Rigid Rule Enforcement **Ethnocentric Orientations:** - US-Centric Lens Encouraged: "Our Way or the Highway"	**Cross-Cultural Competence:** - Multicultural Worldview: Sufficient Cultural Relativism - Humanize / Sensitivity: Develop Commonality, Trust, Relationships - Listen to, Follow, Work with, Learn About and From Diverse People **Build/Teach:** - Mentor, Teach, Train, Advise - Build/Preserve/Sustain - Empower Diverse People & Units **Political Agent:** - Diplomat/Ambassador **Adaptability/Suppleness:** - Stretch Rules: Unconventional Tasks - Agency: Invent/Create
Archetype	**General George Patton**	**General David Petreaus**

skills. The sharp contrast between these cultural orientations enhances comprehension of the organizational ambivalence—including pockets of resistance—toward the rise of softer peacekeeper-diplomat cultural developments. This conceptual snapshot does not seek to argue that military culture boils down to this simplistic model, but rather this comparison aims to isolate these two prominent facets of contemporary military culture to illuminate their intriguing contradictory qualities for this paper.

An important component of emergent postmodern military culture and especially the peacekeeper-diplomat cultural orientations and toolset that possesses enormous applicability in the advising mission consists of cross-cultural competence.[5] Professional cultural orientations in the US military enable the organization to effectively rise above bureaucratic rigidity and resistance toward softer skill development (linked to a defense of the traditional warrior cultural core) to create essential new cultural tools, such as cross-cultural competence. This article defines cross-cultural competence as the knowledge, attitudes, and behavioral repertoire and skill sets that military members require to accomplish all given tasks and missions in situations marked by substantial cultural diversity. Cross-cultural competence consists of two major subparts: culture-general factors and culture-specific factors. The culture-general factors constitute the foundation of cross-cultural competence for the military, consisting of the core attitudes, skill sets, and knowledge basis that facilitate adaptation to multiple culturally diverse contexts over time. The culture-specific factors of cross-cultural competence consist of the necessary attitudes, skills, and knowledge sets that enable effective mission performance in a given assignment characterized by significant cultural diversity, such as the case of advising in a specific place. The military works to develop both components of cross-cultural competence, including the culture-general and the culture-specific factors, to successfully carry out its requirements in the contemporary landscape. In sum, these pertinent sources of interdisciplinary literature coalesce to form an overarching theoretical framework (e.g., postmodern military culture with a primary focus on the warrior–peacekeeper-diplomat and cross-cultural competence spheres) to launch this project's investigation of defining military advising success.

Method

I applied a three-part multimethod to conduct this research project. The first major part of the study consisted of collection and analysis of data gathered in extremis in Iraq from September 2009 to March 2010. The most substantial data collected in Iraq comes from a survey conducted in a US advisory unit in January to February 2010, which included input from twenty-three participants. Sixteen subjects served as advisors and seven served as linguists. Eight participants had previous advisor experiences worldwide prior to serving as an advisor in Iraq. Although most of the survey data focused on the subjects' advising experiences in Iraq, veteran advisor participants also reported relevant data beyond Iraq (e.g., global context, peacetime conditions, different kinds of missions, etc.). While in Iraq, I also collected a report of Iraqi counterparts' input about US advisors that was prepared by an Iraqi scholar as well as advisor training materials and field notes, all of which yielded relevant data.

The second major part of the multimethod involved gathering and analyzing military journal articles, monographs, book chapters, US military doctrine, and advisor classes (training). This data provided a broader perspective to the overall dataset, including insights from around the world, different kinds of advising units (e.g., different military branches and specialties), a historic context[6] (Ramsey 2006; Stoker 2008), peacetime and wartime advising situations, diverse types of advisors, distinctive advising missions, and other variations. In sum, the breadth and uniqueness from the document data complemented the other two major parts of the multimethod, which produced a fuller and more intricate overall dataset.

The third major prong of the multimethod constituted eleven semi-structured interviews conducted in December 2011 to January 2012. I conducted ten interviews with current or former advisors and one interview with a former linguist. I recorded and transcribed these interviews that lasted between 47 and 155 minutes (average length of about ninety minutes). The strength of this third group of interview data consists of the depth of relevant answers provided by the informants. Having conducted the first two portions of the multimethod and some data analysis prior to the interview phase, I was prepared with focused questions and ready to spontaneously ask pointed follow-on questions to capture fresh insights and new angles, explore pertinent ambiguities, suitably approach potentially controversial topics, and seek corroboration for, or contradictory, insights (Miles and Huberman 1994). Although the interview data provided triangulation for most of the findings emanating from the Iraq and document data, some noteworthy new insights produced greater richness and sophistication in the project's results.

In conclusion, three major subparts of the research multimethod provided a fruitful dataset. The first prong yielded different forms of data collected in Iraq, particularly the useful Iraq survey data (N = 23 subjects). The second part of the multimethod produced germane and broadening advising document data (N = 20), including journal articles, monographs, military doctrine, and book chapters. The third aspect of the multimethod yielded eleven in-depth semistructured interviews with advisors and a linguist, which provided salient, distinctive, contradictory, and complementary data. The initial analysis of the Iraq data yielded initial categories, conceptual clusters, and trends, which expanded in complexity during the reiterative analytical processes that occurred throughout the project. Triangulation of the results from these three distinct data sources strengthened the findings' overall validity and reliability. Despite the strengths of the multimethod, it had some limitations. First, data from post-9/11 Iraq and Afghanistan advising missions take center stage, although some of the survey, document, and interview data provide broader historical and regional perspectives. Second, despite attempts to not allow my personal advising experiences in Iraq to overly impact my analysis and interpretation of the data, it is reasonable to assume that in some cases my efforts fell short.

Findings: The Swiss Army Knife of Advisory Skills

This section summarizes the project's major findings and sets the stage for a main concentration on defining military advising success. An informant uses the metaphor of a "Swiss Army knife," which serves as a fitting symbol for the cultural toolkit deployed by contemporary advisors to conduct their mission. Switzerland's reputation for neutrality and peace makes the combination of the word "Swiss" (peacekeeper-diplomat) with the words "Army knife" (warrior) extremely suitable for this article's conceptual design and argument. A sledgehammer would symbolize the military's historic combat warrior identity, which evolved to include smaller hammers, scalpels, other kinds of knife blades, and new tools needed for different kinds of combat missions of varying intensities. The contemporary "Swiss Army knife" also includes emerging peacekeeper-diplomat, information age technology, soft and hard leader skills, expertise, and other tools required to perform a full spectrum of noncombat and combat operations. Advisors draw from their Swiss Army knives to traverse numerous complexities, balancing acts, dangers, and ambiguities that characterize the contemporary advising tightrope.

Although this article primarily discusses the study's finding about how advisors conceive mission success,[7] a brief synopsis of the project's other major findings provides a necessary broader context. One main finding includes the significance of advisors effectively building relationships with foreign counterparts (Hajjar 2014b). Another major finding discusses the important role of linguists in the advising mission; solid advisor-linguist relationships serve as a prerequisite for advisors to forge strong ties with foreign counterparts. Two other larger intertwined findings disclosed advising as an unconventional and second-tier mission given the task's unusual in-depth cross-cultural requirements and the mission's lower status compared to traditional command roles and combat functions. As the mainstream military adapted to conduct the unconventional advising mission in Iraq and Afghanistan after 9/11, many advisors practiced tremendous creativity and agency by stretching boundaries (and in turn causing ripples of cultural change) in the conventional military to spend sufficient time with, operate alongside, and at times live on counterpart bases. Finally, an amalgamation of other patterns emerged, including the role of information age technology, the importance of relevant subject matter expertise, the provision of various "goodies" (e.g., equipment, shared intelligence, and so on) to counterparts, considerations for deploying woman advisors, and the need to successfully interact with various actors in the advising environment.

Defining Military Advising Success

This section discusses the findings regarding defining US military advising success. One core pattern that emerges constitutes the difficulty for advisors to pin down success. An interrogation of the dataset exposes the ambiguity, messiness, and contradictory views about the nature of the mission and the challenges of defining advisory achievement. Amidst this confusion, a few relatively coherent trends emerge regarding defining advisory success. One finding this report explores, "Iraqi (or Afghan) Good Enough," superficially appears to bear an ethnocentric outlook. However, this theme actually reveals open-mindedness, tolerance, flexibility, perspective taking, and cross-culturally competent advisors. A second finding constitutes advisors who frame success as working themselves out of a job, meaning they have helped counterparts to achieve a level of professional competence and autonomy whereby counterparts no longer need advisors. This second pattern often emerges in cases where advisors recognize the military's imminent withdrawal from a host nation, such as in the latter phases of Iraq and Afghanistan. Establishing enduring relationships with counterparts surfaces as the third major trend regarding how advisors conceive success, which serves as an intangible measure of accomplishment in a mission that often lacks conspicuous, tangible, and objective signs of progress. This section explains how these core themes contribute to a definition of success in the nebulous, unconventional, postmodern, and contemporary US military advising mission.

In the first account, Don, an informant, views the growing independence of his counterpart as a sign of success.

> Let me say a couple things about how you know if you're being successful. *A huge measure of success is when they're out doin' stuff on their own.* It's kinda counterintuitive, but it's almost good to find out about something after the fact because then you're like, they didn't frickin' come to me and say they need fuel [or] say they needed anything, they just went and did [an operation]. That's what my guy's [Afghan counterpart] doin' a lot, and I feel good about that. I think it's a good measure of success (Don, forty-two, three advising experiences worldwide, advisor and team leader in Afghanistan; emphasis added).

Don views the growing autonomy of his counterpart and Afghan police unit as a "huge measure of success." He notes it may seem "counterintuitive" to some US advisors that it is "good to find out about something (a military operation) after the fact," meaning that he feels some advisors might react negatively if they discover "after the fact" that their counterpart unit conducted military operations. In Don's case, we can sense his relief about his counterpart's rising independence: "[T] hey didn't frickin' come to me and say they need fuel or anything, they just went and did it (the operation)." Don "feels pretty good about" his counterpart's growing autonomy, which supports a finding for advisors (like Don) who sense an approaching US military departure from the host nation.

Don also discussed an advising technique of unobtrusive presence, which he reports produced a form of advising mission success.

> He (Afghan counterpart, police chief) has 32 checkpoint commanders that work for him across the district. It's one of the most robust and successful police districts. In fact, it will be the second district to go independent in terms of just police securing the district. Because *he knows I listen to what's goin' on and I'm tied in to what's goin' on, when he's making a decision about something with his commanders there he'll ask for my opinion.* I don't think he would do that if he didn't think I was paying attention to what's going on. To me that's the most effective approach because the Afghans, it's a much different culture than our culture. So *Americans don't like to sit around with them; they don't feel comfortable.* There are guys on my team that I'm constantly after, "Hey, you gotta get more contact time. You gotta just be there." They get frustrated because they'll go and they'll say, "Here's how you should do something" (Don, forty-two, three advising tours globally, advisor and team leader in Afghanistan; emphasis added)

Don discusses another form of advisory success he experienced with his Afghan counterpart who serves as a district chief of police. Through

Don's daily presence and his counterpart's knowledge that Don "listens" and is "tied in to what's goin' on" in the police district headquarters, his counterpart often asks for Don's opinion when making operational decisions. In our interview, Don says sometimes his CP will apply Don's recommendations even when they contradict the plans that the Afghan counterpart police chief originally had in mind. Although Don frames his counterpart soliciting and listening to advice as a positive outcome of an effective advisory approach, this idea differs from his previous narrative in which he painted cases where his counterpart would independently conduct operations and inform Don "after the fact" as a sign of success. Although on the surface these ideas may seem contrasting, Don defines both developments as different kinds of success. Specifically, the reported gradual increase in Don's counterpart's autonomy and initiative during his eight months of work with his counterpart provides a strategic indicator of development and growth. The increased counterpart independence presumably partially resulted from the effectual daily interactions between Don and his counterpart.

Importantly, the informant reflects on the significance of peacekeeper-diplomat tools such as culture-specific competence (Afghan culture is a "much different culture than ours"), patience, and a more subdued, unobtrusive, yet keenly aware advisory method based on presence. Don says he attempts to influence his advisor subordinates to apply this approach, but he observes, "Americans don't like to sit around with them; they don't feel comfortable." Soldiers prefer to take action and show counterparts, "here's how you should do something." These insights reinforce the finding that successful advisors draw on softer, peacekeeper-diplomat cultural tools (patience, observation, waiting for counterparts to ask questions) and judiciously apply warrior tools (e.g., forcefulness, rigidity). Don relays his advisor subordinates' missteps by discussing their culturally ingrained predilections for taking action, giving commands and instructions, and bearing conventional military conformist orientations, all of which illustrate classic warrior tools that if used at unsuitable times tend to cause advisory failure or reduced effectiveness.

The following US military doctrinal guidance discusses military advising goals and success.

DESIRED *END STATE*. Training Host Nation security forces is a *slow and painstaking process.* It does not lend itself to a "quick fix." Real success does not appear as a single decisive victory. To ensure long-term success, commanders clarify their desired end state for training programs early. This end state consists of a *set of characteristics common to all militaries.* Those characteristics have nuances in different countries, but well-trained host nation security forces should: provide reasonable levels of security from external threats while not threatening regional security; provide reasonable levels of internal security without infringing upon the populace's civil liberties or posing a coup threat; be founded upon the rule of law; and be sustainable by the host nation after U.S. and multinational forces depart (United States Government 2006: 6; emphasis added).

This doctrinal passage reinforces several trends in the study. The passage discusses the "slow and painstaking process" of advising and training foreign forces and states that these processes do not involve a "single decisive victory," which links to a theme in the current study. Further, the objective for counterpart units "to be sustainable by the host nation after U.S. and multinational forces depart" also contributes to my finding. The discussion of a "set" of ideals that "commonly" apply "to all militaries" carries an aura of US military conformist and ethnocentric cultural orientations, despite the doctrine's recognition that "those characteristics have different nuances in different countries." Whether or not a foreign security force eventually endorses a "rule of law," honors "civil liberties," and remains an effective security instrument that does not pose a "coup" or "regional security" threat (in ways that the United States or the West envision these cultural values), all link to overarching host nation structural and cultural factors that stretch beyond military advisors' sphere of influence or scope of responsibility. Nonetheless, trends in the results reveal advisors encourage counterparts to conduct less detainee abuse, build better civil-military relations, develop a legal system where a "rule of law" dictates how to prosecute captured alleged enemies and criminals, become more autonomous, and gradually move in the direction of these ideals.

One of the tricky, unstated, and inherently ambiguous points associated with these lofty and idealistic advising and nation-building objectives entails the need for advisors (as well as diplomats and other actors working toward these initiatives) to gain comfort in tolerating the actual counterpart and host nation governmental practices. The counterpart military's culture and modus operandi oftentimes fall short of these grand doctrinal models. Subsequently, successful advisors accept "Iraqi (or any counterpart) Good Enough" performance standards; hence, advisors require cognitive flexibility, cultural stretching, and the ability to understand and tolerate a counterpart unit's idiosyncratic history and current conditions to assess counterpart capabilities and form realistic performance objectives. Thus, part of the advising balancing act consists of advisors who simultaneously practice open-minded acceptance of daily counterpart practices (the exception being when nonnegotiable moral boundaries get crossed, such as detainee abuse) and who also diplomatically nudge and influence counterparts to gradually adopt new beneficial cultural orientations and skills that realistically align with aspects of the doctrinally stated vision for the host nation and counterpart military.

Finally, the use of the words "end state" in the passage provides a noteworthy contradiction to the "slow and painstaking process" of advising. "End state" implies that, by the end of advisory efforts, the host nation will realize the overarching doctrinal objectives and ideals. However, Iraq and Afghanistan constitute clear examples in which US advisory efforts have significantly waned, yet the counterpart security force and host-nation building will continue long into the future, which reveals the myth of a definitive "end state." Thus, the seemingly forced misapplication of a popular contemporary U.S. military concept—"end state"—yields a conspicuous contradiction that subtly divulges another sign that the military struggles to comprehend the elusive definition of success in the unconventional military advising mission.

After serving as an advisor in Iraq for two years, in response to a survey, Oliver wrote the following two accounts to explain his views on advisory success in early 2010:

> *Successful and effective advising gains Iraqi personal friendships to last a lifetime.* Yeah, a lifetime: For Christmas I got a text message from one of the [counterparts] wishing me "Happy Christmas." I went over to meet with S.COL [Iraqi staff colonel] Samir and he gave me out of the blue a very nice glass table piece that has some historical pictures on it as a gift. *Success is when they say, "We need you,"* "We would like to see you," "Where have you been?," etc. Success as an advisor is when you give them honest effort and offer them realism.
>
> *"Success:"* Some look to mission success indicators for where we are; however, for me, the only thing that is valid at this point in time is *proper transitioning of Iraqis for self-sustainment.* U.S. must learn to let go as we draw closer to leaving. If we do not, we will inadvertently set them up for failure or leave them 'hanging' as we depart without completing the new venture. This is not about one year tours for some sort of career accolade; it is about the lives of Iraqi civilians in a theater of hostilities that will continue "the war" after we leave (Oliver, thirty-five, military advisor in Iraq; emphasis added).

This subject defines advisory "success" in both a tactical, short-term, and microlevel manner as well as a strategic, long-term, and macrolevel framing. The first narrative provides Oliver's microlevel reflections about his relationships and "personal friendships" with Iraqi counterparts that will "last a lifetime," which links to the finding where advisors define success through enduring relationships with counterparts.

The subject relayed how a counterpart surprised him with a "Happy Christmas" text and gift and that his counterpart told him, "We need you" and "We would like to see you." Oliver reports that an advisor's "honest effort" to provide a counterpart with "realism" fortifies a relationship and leads to advisory success. It seems the counterpart perceived Oliver's relevance and competence, which an Iraqi study of U.S. advisors underscores as vital. Although my analysis of a report produced by a retired Iraqi general officer about US advisors leaves me skeptical of the scientific soundness of the study, I will mention the report's finding that only 50% of US advisors provided useful suggestions to their Iraqi counterparts. Thus, for advisors to succeed in the eyes of their counterparts, they must possess salient expertise and actively provide useful recommendations to their advisees.

The second passage illustrates the finding that advisors define success by helping counterparts to "self-sustain" as the United States prepares to depart from the host nation, which constitutes a grander, strategic definition of advisory success. Further, Oliver maintains that the main point of advising does not involve bolstering advisors' "careers" but rather safeguarding the well-being of "Iraqi civilians" who will continue to experience "hostilities" and "the war" after the U.S. military departs. Oliver foretold the importance of preparing Iraqi security forces to operate effectively and independently given the U.S. military's departure from Iraq at the end of 2011. Indeed, in light of recent events, it remains to be seen whether Iraq will defeat substantial internal threats, stabilize, seat a sustainable government, and implement new national systems. In sum, Oliver's comments support themes of advisory success that include developing enduring relationships with counterparts and helping counterparts gain proficiency and autonomy—especially as advisors prepare to withdraw from a host nation.

In the next narrative, Mike, a retired US Special Forces officer, reflects on some successes and some setbacks from his time as an active duty military advisor in Zimbabwe and South Korea.

There's no definitive yardstick or criteria for success. You can anecdotally say yes, I was successful with my counterpart and my sphere of foreign officers and NCOs [noncommissioned officers] I interacted with. However, I know that my [US Special Forces] battalion commander and others within the staff had created some friction with the Zimbabwean military. So, it's a nuanced answer. Did Flintlock Program [a military exchange program between the US and participating African countries] shut down because of what we did? No. Did we have issues in outlying countries with ODAs [Special Forces members] who got into trouble with local authorities and the military? Yea. So all in all it was successful, but there's gonna be issues because of the nature of the operation. It's not centralized; it's guys scattered in five or six different countries doing things. This is speaking from the perspective of our Special Forces battalion at that time. *I felt that our jumpmaster* [training provided by the informant's unit to the Zimbabwean military] *outcome was successful. No injuries, high graduation rate; I felt we had good relations with our folks* [counterparts and students]. We did have a small minority of 'onesies' and 'two-sies,' guys who I thought were not suitable, who we had to reposition. Nothing happened to them; you could just see I need to nip this in the bud before it becomes an issue. The Korean experience, for me, it was personally outstanding. *Korea went well; I'm still in contact with some of my friends [counterparts] from over there* (Mike, fifty-one, retired US Special Forces officer, multiple advisor experiences worldwide, reflections from experiences as an active duty military advisor during an interview; emphasis added).

This passage supports some of the themes regarding conceiving of advisory success, and it also provides some new insights. Mike discusses a peacetime environment in Africa with somewhat of a training flavor, such as the "jumpmaster" course in Zimbabwe that he led, in which he defined success as "no injuries, a high graduate rate, and good relations with our folks [Zimbabwean counterparts and students]." Mike conceptualizes a grander framing of advisory success that also takes failures and tensions into account. The subject reflects on the "frictions" between his own "Special Forces battalion" and the counterpart's, including a few cases where US military members got into trouble in "different African countries," as well as when he occasionally needed to remove inappropriate US advisors and trainers ("onesies" and "two-sies") to "nip things in the bud before it becomes an issue" (for example, as reported later in the interview, one case involved a sergeant who too aggressively yelled at African counterparts and students). Mike also discusses his long-term relationships with South Korean counterparts, saying, "I'm still in contact with some of my friends from over there." Highlighting such lasting relationships with counterparts is another way to frame advisory success, reinforcing this study's finding.

In the next passage, Mike discusses his experiences as a military advisor and trainer while serving as a civilian contractor after his formal retirement from the U.S. military.

I think the Rwanda experience was interesting and successful. *We got follow-on jobs after that, not only in Rwanda but in other parts of Africa. So from the [civilian contracting] company's perspective it was successful,* and I felt good about what we were doing. Peacekeeping mission, this is something I personally felt is a good use for this force. The Rwandans had a tough go of it back in the 90s; this is a chance for them to redeem themselves. Some of the staff officers I had worked with and commanders were part of the warring factions back in the '95 -'96 timeframe. I think we were successful in that regard (Mike, fifty-one, retired US Special Forces officer, multiple advisor experiences worldwide, reflections from experiences as a civilian contractor military advisor during an interview; emphasis added).

Mike's reflections about how he defined advisory success while serving as a civilian contractor both reinforce a pattern in the dataset and also introduce new themes. One finding in the study entailed advisors' efforts to help counterparts develop better relations with their civilian populations, including reducing counterparts' participation in and tolerance for human rights abuses. The subject's comments about how his advising mission in Rwanda provided his counterparts a chance to "redeem themselves" by learning how to conduct "peacekeeping missions" struck him as fitting given the violence linked to the "warring factions back in the '95 –'96 time frame." Mike's insight supports the idea of advisors influencing counterparts to adopt orientations and skills that improve civil-military relations and reduce civilian abuses inflicted by the host nation's security forces.

Mike introduces a fresh theme from a profit-seeking civilian contractor perspective when he explains how the "follow on jobs" in "Rwanda and different countries in Africa" (when his contractor company earned new business contracts) constituted a form of advisory success. His discussion of how his civilian business "company" sought profits through new contracts in Africa as a for-profit measure of success stands out as one of the most explicit data sources in the study that reveals this perspective. Field notes from my experiences as an advisor and deputy advisory team leader in Iraq where I worked with numerous advisor and linguist civilian contractors support this finding. My reflections from Iraq include impressions of civilian contractor teammates who generally worked hard and performed well, but who also possessed a strong monetary motivation. A few contractor colleagues discussed their compensations with me, although salary generally constituted an off-limits topic. I recall a linguist contractor who explained that about $95,000 (US) of his wage was tax-free because he served in a combat theater, which generated a much larger net salary from his approximate $155,000 annual wage.

This finding regarding how civilian contractor advisor team members define success exposes a noteworthy difference in how diverse advisors frame advisory success. On the one hand, many active duty advisors report success as "working themselves out of a job" as they help counterparts gain competence and autonomy, which signals a strong motivation to accomplish the main purpose of the advising mission. This indicates an institutional orientation toward performing military service (Moskos and Wood 1988). On the other hand, advisor and linguist contractors who view monetary compensation as their primary incentive to work provide evidence for an occupational orientation (Moskos and Wood 1988; Kelty and Segal 2007; Kelty and Bierman 2013). The 2011 drawdown in Iraq, for example, forced thousands of military contractors working in advisor, linguist, and other roles to find new employment amidst a global recession where in the vast majority of cases I deduce their prospects of finding comparable salaries were improbable. In sum, another definition for advisory success in the postmodern military (that includes large numbers of civilian contractors) constitutes the retention of employment through "follow on jobs" and new contracts, which contrasts the finding of active duty advisors who report trying to "work themselves out of a job" by building counterparts' capabilities and independence.[8]

A military advisor in Iraq reflected on his experiences in *Military Review*, the professional journal for the US Army (Deady 2009). His comments contribute to the study's "Iraqi Good Enough" theme.

> *"Iraqi Good Enough."* While the term "Iraqi good enough" might sound pejorative, it simply acknowledges that one cannot realistically use U.S. Army metrics such as Unit Status Report ratings, Mission Essential Task List proficiency, or Army Training and Evaluation Program standards in measuring success in building the Iraqi Army. The phrase represents the coalition's attempt to quantify how proficient the Iraqi Army needs to become. Speaking of Afghanistan, the commander of the Combined Security Transition Command stated, "We don't need to make these cops as good as the 82nd Airborne. *We need to make them two-and-a-half times better than the enemy."* While one can quantify and compare elements of combat power between symmetric forces [in conventional warfare], it is awkward to quantify the effectiveness of the Iraqi Army over its insurgent and militia enemies [in nontraditional, asymmetric warfare]. T.E. Lawrence counseled, "Better the Arabs do it tolerably than that you do it for them." Advisors tempted to insert themselves into an Iraqi operation should always reconsider Lawrence's advice before acting. If an event meets "Iraqi good enough" standards, it is normally better to let it continue without interruption and later address concerns and recommendations in an after-action review. Inserting coalition force [advisor] solutions, particularly as an [Iraqi counterpart] operation is unfolding, risks undermining the confidence that comes with proficiency (Deady 2009: 54–55; emphasis added).

This account articulates the "Iraqi Good Enough" pattern in the study, where the word "Iraqi" represents any given counterpart. The passage talks about this concept's relevance in Iraq and Afghanistan; one general declared that as long as Afghan police forces became "two and half times better than the enemy," that would satisfy their security needs. This declaration reveals a necessary open-mindedness, understanding of nuanced counterpart situations, and tolerance for counterpart performance standards that may fall below US military standards (such as those of the "Eighty-Second Airborne" Division) but simultaneously creates new uncertainties, such as determining what being "two and half times better than the (nontraditional, asymmetric) enemy" means.

Citing renowned British military advisor T. E. Lawrence, the narrative states that advisors should not interrupt counterparts when they independently plan and conduct operations in a "tolerable" manner because this autonomous action helps counterparts to build "confidence" and "proficiency." Thus, advisors should not forcefully "insert themselves into" their counterpart's mission preparations, which requires advisors to subdue their command and their take charge cultural orientations. The article suggests advisors should exercise patience and provide "recommendations" for improvement to counterparts after the completion of an operation. In sum, this passage supports the finding of how "Iraqi (or Afghan) Good Enough" encompasses an effective advisory approach that constitutes an open-minded and flexible method to gauge counterpart performance and contemporary advising success.

The following passage provides further details and support for the "Iraqi Good Enough" finding.

> *The Iraqi Army troops learned to use American tactics but with Iraqi twists.* The differences in manning, equipment, and leadership culture generated these differences. For instance, while conducting cache searches, the Iraqis lacked technical equipment, so when operating independently they used different, more rudimentary search techniques until they started getting technical equipment of their own. Likewise, Iraqi Army leaders, especially at the lieutenant [junior officer] level, configured operations slightly differently so that they could personally control different aspects of the operation rather than coordinate and command subordinates. The Iraqis became basically proficient in their operations, sometimes doing well, and other times barely clearing the bar. In the final analysis, *the Iraqi Army's role requires them to be marginally better than the insurgents and terrorists. . . .* [T]hey met that criterion (Grube 2008: 222; emphasis added).

The passage talks about the "Iraqi twists" regarding "differences in manning, equipment, and leadership culture." The advisor accepts a mixed level of counterpart performance that includes "basic proficiency" and some cases where counterparts "barely cleared the bar." The narrative explains that "the Iraqi Army's role requires them to be marginally better than the insurgents and terrorists," and the advisor concluded the counterparts "met that criterion;" thus, in this case "Iraqi Good Enough" means possessing the capability to suppress security threats to Iraq. The final interesting aspect of the account entails how the "Iraqi Army" unit modified its operational procedures by making them more "rudimentary" in cases where it did not possess the highly "technical" equipment (that the US military possesses). In sum, this article explains how advisors defined satisfactory counterpart performance as possessing the capability to meet Iraq's nuanced security needs, which reinforces the "Iraqi Good Enough" finding.

A senior US military advisor with experiences in Iraq and Afghanistan provided the following reflections about defining success in contemporary advising missions.

> We have had a lot of success. The Afghans are training independently now. Tactical operations, we're always partnered with them, but they're taking initiative to plan and execute now. It depends on what kind of operation it is and where it is, and *they always rely on us for the enablers. That's kinda the strategy* as we drawdown; we'll continue to do that as we provide them access to helicopters, fires, and so forth. That one is very much on track, particularly with the [Afghan] Army. The [Afghan] police, we've got a ways to go. But we see glimmers of hope every day; they take the initiative, for instance. They respond to emergencies, whether it's a roadside bomb that's been discovered or it's a rocket or something that hits and impacts some place in their jurisdiction, they send a patrol out there. Having them take the initiative and not wait for us to coach them or show them what needs to be done. Again it gets back to whether we help them help themselves. I think it's important that we recognize that they may do things in a way that we wouldn't. *If it works for them, and you have some modicum of success doing it that way, even if it's not the way you'd [U.S. military] do it, we need to be satisfied.* Otherwise we'll never get out of there, and the same for Iraq. We need to be OK, provided that they're not torturing people, they're not killing people, they're not stealing, things like that. An operation that they're doing that doesn't look like the way we would do it, we just need to accept it and to be supportive. My point is we are seeing those kinda things—we're seeing progress (Ted, fifty, military advisor in Iraq and Afghanistan, senior advisory supervisor in Afghanistan; emphasis added)

Ted's reflections contribute to the "Iraqi (or Afghan) Good Enough" theme and provide some additional insights. He states that if advisors do not learn to accept that counterparts will do "an operation" in ways that do not "look like the way we would do it," then "we'll never get out of there"—referring to Afghanistan and Iraq. As the informant paints an "Iraqi Good Enough" picture, he draws a line regarding advisors not tolerating the crossing of certain moral boundaries, such as counterparts "torturing people," "killing people," and "stealing." Although he acknowledges that Afghan police still have "got a ways to go" in their development, Ted mentions some "glimmers" of success in the budding Afghan police whereby they more frequently "take the initiative" and respond to "roadside bombs," "rockets," and other incidences that "impact some place in their jurisdiction" without first getting "coached" by their advisors. This supports the assumption of advisors who define success as counterparts operating more autonomously, which becomes relevant for advisors who will soon withdraw from a host nation. Ted also mentions advisors providing counterparts access to US "helicopters," "fires," and other "enablers" to bolster counterpart operations as part of a successful advising "strategy." This point of view raises the question of how the Afghan security forces will fare without the support of "enablers" after the US withdraws, which casts some doubts over the establishment of Afghan counterpart independence. In sum, Ted's main point is that advisors must learn to accept counterpart performance as long as it produces a "modicum of success" because doing so encourages counterpart independence. Thus, Ted's portrayal of advisory success contributes to the "Iraqi Good Enough" pattern and other findings.

The next informant served twice as an advisor in Iraq, and he explains the process of trying to assess advising success as messy, uncertain, intuitive, and intangible:

> *How do you properly establish metrics for a foreign culture* when you're trying to accomplish something? Do you revert back to what you can reasonably expect of the American? Do you invent a completely new metric or methodology for assessment? How do we assess the level that [counterpart] organization "A" is at? Whether that's the operational readiness assessment or the ability to do drill and ceremonies, that is the *art aspect.* We try to apply our military science solutions . . . really, *a gut feeling might be a better assessment than a bunch of statistics* (Todd, thirty-nine, two military advising tours in Iraq; emphasis added).

In this interview, Todd discusses the complicated challenges linked to measuring advisory success and counterpart proficiency. First, he explains the conundrum involved in assessing the counterpart's performance when he asks whether the US military should "invent a completely new metric or methodology for assessment." Second, his narrative reinforces a pattern regarding hyperconformist tendencies in the conventional US military when he contemplates how to assess counterparts and asks, "Do you revert back to what you can reasonably expect of the American (service member)?" Indeed, this reveals that the effectual "Iraqi Good Enough" advisory approach counters the idea of expecting counterparts to meet US military performance standards. Finally, Todd also critiques the military's excessive application of "military science" in trying to "properly establish metrics for a foreign culture," arguing that "a gut feeling might be a better assessment than a bunch of statistics." Indeed, the informant's suggestion that the best method to "assess" counterparts may very well involve advisors who artistically apply their intuition or "gut feelings" implies that advisors not only need relevant military experience and expertise but also keen situational awareness of the counterpart's capabilities and overarching circumstances. This implies a kind of "I know success when I see it" approach toward assessing counterparts. The informant's insights explain the complications and messiness linked to defining advisory success, which is particularly the case for the assessment of counterpart units' capabilities.

Todd's reflections become more personal when he responds to a question regarding his perceptions of his own success as a military advisor.

> *I think I was a good combat advisor.* I think I definitely made an impact on the [Iraqi] organization. *I can't tell you if I was successful or not.* I felt a lot of successes, and I felt a lot of frustrations. Did I find it one of the most rewarding experiences of my life? Absolutely. Did I meet Iraqis in '05 and '06 that, when I came back in '09 and [when] I saw them again for the first time, they ran up and hugged me; they were so happy to see me? Absolutely. *Did that make me successful? I have no idea. No clue. I don't think that's an answerable question.* I think I was a good advisor; I think I was probably better than most at being a combat advisor. But *I can't tell you if I was successful or not* (Todd, thirty-nine, two military advising tours in Iraq; emphasis added).

Reflecting on whether he personally succeeded as an advisor, Todd recalled Iraqi counterparts who knew him in 2005–2006 and who "ran up and hugged" him because "they were so happy to see" him when he returned. However, he does not know if this event and the implied positive relationship between Todd and his former counterparts mean he succeeded as an advisor. Despite the fact that he believes he "was a good combat advisor" who was "probably better than most" and who "made an impact on the (Iraqi) organization," Todd concludes on an uncertain note by asserting that he has "no clue" if he was "successful." This supports the theme of the inherent ambiguity and haziness in the mission, as well as the difficulty in gauging advising success. Todd's reflections also contribute to an emerging trend whereby advisors view enduring relationships with counterparts as an informal, intangible, and meaningful measure of success.

Conclusion

The findings of this study regarding how best to conceive of advisory success involve numerous subthemes and bring to light the contradictory, fuzzy, incoherent, ambiguous, and elusive nature of attempting to define success in the unconventional advising mission, which bears postmodern qualities. Indeed, "Iraqi (any counterpart) Good Enough" surfaces as a main theme, which means advisors seek to help their counterparts perform at a level that meets the host nation's security requirements (but does not mechanically focus on US military standards). Despite some attempts by the US military to tangibly and objectively measure counterpart performance, advisors reported difficulties in attempting to conduct such "scientific" assessments, especially in combat conditions.

As one informant reported, advisors' artistic application of subjective "gut feelings" best assesses counterpart performance. This highlights a theme about the conventional US military's problematic attempts to apply highly precise measurements in its evaluations of counterpart proficiency and progress. Thus, the military could benefit by learning to accept more subjective appraisals from veteran combat advisors about counterpart capabilities, performance, progress, and potential.

As noted in this study, many advisors framed advisory success as "working themselves out of a job," meaning they helped counterparts achieve a level of professional competence whereby advisors became unnecessary. This answer often emerges in tandem with advisors who recognize the imminent US military withdrawal from a host nation. Thus, while the study reveals that civilian contractor advisors and linguists bring relevant expertise and a good work ethic to the mission, their motivation for continued employment (often at a much higher compensation level than most contractors would otherwise receive) calls into question whether they genuinely wish to "work themselves out of a job" (Kelty and Bierman 2013). This dichotomy in the findings illuminates how the postmodern US military's diverse members and advisors may frame success differently.

Another major finding consists of advisors who define success by establishing enduring relationships with counterparts. Some advisors reported returning to a host nation and visiting former counterparts, emphasizing that both the advisors and counterparts enjoyed the reunion. Other advisors reported receiving gifts, holiday greetings, and other forms of generosity (as, for example, invitations to feasts and celebrations), calls for future visits by advisors, and other such positive perceived indications of a strong, lasting relationship and friendship.

Thus, given the fact that the advising mission lacks concrete and objective measures of military success linked to traditional combat, such as battles won, enemies defeated, structures or vehicles destroyed, and land taken, the findings reveal how advisors create intangible and subjective ways to gauge success, including "gut feelings" about counterparts' capabilities and building long-term relationships and friendships with counterparts. We can conclude that such informal signs of success help advisors negotiate the vagueness and uncertainties of mission progress. Moreover, these intangible indicators of achievement carry even greater value and significance of meaning for advisors given their work in a large organization that expects and respects more concrete and tangible measures of success.

Finally, the findings reveal how advisors draw on their elaborate Swiss Army knives to accomplish their mission, including defining success. Advisors draw on peacekeeper-diplomat tools, such as culture-specific competence (a keen understanding of counterparts and conditions, diplomacy, patience, flexibility, and perspective taking), innovativeness (including creating advisory work tasks and measures for success), subdued warrior tools (by avoiding to command or demand conformity, applying relevant combat skills, and exhibiting polite firmness when appropriate), subject matter expertise (to impart vital skills and assess counterparts), and other such tools to help counterparts gain autonomy and build capability. In conclusion, the complexity of defining advisory success not only reveals the ambiguity inherent in a prominent contemporary military mission but also reveals the emergence of a postmodern US military.

Theoretical Implications

The findings reveal that contemporary advisors negotiate, create, and contribute to myriad tensions, contradictions, ambiguities, and distinctive organizational cultural spheres of influence as they conduct their unconventional mission, which divulges emergent postmodern US military culture. Advisors draw on a dynamic advisory cultural toolkit (see figure 4) to accomplish the mission, including inventing ways to frame success. A repertoire of essential cultural tools, including warrior (courage, appropriate forcefulness and command orientations, combat skills and experience), peacekeeper-diplomat (diplomacy, cross-cultural competence, flexibility, and mentorship), leader, subject matter expert, persuasion (mainly through softer forms of power and influence), and robust innovativeness (agency), constituted relevant tools that successful advisors deployed. Regarding cross-cultural competence, this study reveals that open-mindedness, patience, empathy, tolerance, cognitive flexibility, and the ability to rapidly acquire substantial culture-specific competence (e.g., linguist and counterpart nuances, foreign unit circumstances, culture of the host nation, religion, a few key local phrases, and useful cross-cultural skills) all empower advisors to make sound decisions, create new tools, conceive of success, and advance the mission. The most effective advisors demonstrate tremendous agency as they adaptively expand and leverage the space in the seams between their own national and military culture and that of their counterparts. This newly crafted shared cultural space enables advisory teams (e.g.,

Figure 4
Military Advisors' Cultural Toolkit

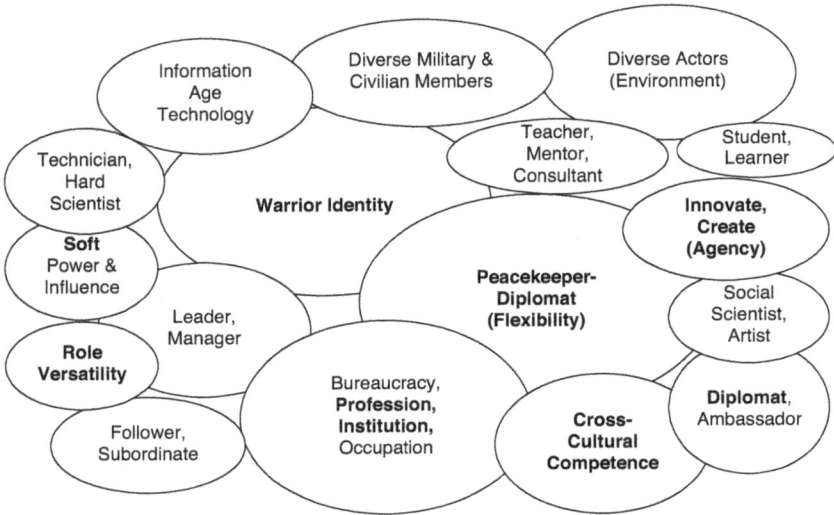

advisors and linguists) to build trust, rapport, and mutual understanding with counterparts, which serves as a gateway for advisors to effectively influence counterparts to become open to learning new skills and ways of operating, and to make beneficial changes.

Therefore, this project reinforces the emergence of postmodern military culture (figure 2), and especially the similar advisory cultural toolkit (figure 4) that draws heavily from the peacekeeper-diplomat and associated cultural spheres to enable advisors to cross cultural bridges, build relationships with linguists and counterparts, define success, and advance the mission. Adapting cultural toolkit theory to the case of the military provides sufficient conceptual space and flexibility for the development and coexistence of seemingly oppositional but vitally necessary cultural spheres, such as the warrior and peacekeeper-diplomat cultural toolsets (figure 3), in the military's culture. The advisory cultural toolkit bears strong resemblance to postmodern military culture, but the advisory toolkit more rigorously cultivates peacekeeper-diplomat, cross-cultural competence, role versatility, soft bases of power and influence, innovativeness (agency), and sufficiently subdued command, conformist, and other warrior tools. Beyond the case of advising, the growing set of contemporary noncombat missions (e.g., a range of peace-oriented operations, infrastructure building, humanitarian assistance and disaster relief, and so on) requiring more intricate and softer cultural orientations produces changes in the organization's culture, which moves the U.S. and other advanced military's modernist cultures toward nascent postmodern military culture and form.[9] Finally, this study reinforces the recommendation to innovate the postmodern military theory by explicitly incorporating a culture variable, which would provide the model with more comprehensive and sharper explanatory power as well as greater overall elegance.[10]

Future Research

This section sets forth some recommendations for future research regarding defining success in the contemporary military advising mission. The advising mission of post-9/11 campaigns in Iraq and Afghanistan clearly takes center stage in this study's findings; thus, future research should seek to explore different missions and regions of the world to assess the nuances of the role in various other contexts. Providing fresh perspectives would corroborate or contradict and, thereby, expand the findings reported in this article on defining advisory success. Further, a systematic examination of international armed forces' lessons learned about how to define advisory success would also constitute worthwhile research. Future studies should also examine the extent to which the equipment, money, materiel, and many other items provided to counterparts actually help *entire* foreign forces and organizations evolve and improve, as opposed to potentially only providing personal gain to individual counterparts (Simmons 2013). These proposals for future studies would not only enhance our understanding of the contemporary military advising mission and how to gauge success, but they would also sharpen our comprehension of the nascent postmodern military and its culture.

Notes

1. This article draws heavily from Hajjar's (2014b) article as a framework to advance findings regarding defining advisory success.
2. This project reveals that active duty US military members, military reservists, National Guardsmen, government civilians (from numerous organizations), and civilian contractors all serve as contemporary US military advisors.
3. The vast majority of cases in this study involve linguists. A very small number of reported cases ensued where the advisor did not utilize a linguist because the foreign counterpart spoke English sufficiently.
4. In figure 1, the bolded lettering in the spheres indicates the roles played by the different actors in the triad. The under lined letters indicate that linguists typically share the national or regional culture of the counterpart. The italicized letters indicate that advisors and some linguists share US culture (although some local national linguists

do not share US culture). The normal lettering indicates the shared military culture between counterparts and advisors; albeit there are important differences in their national and military cultures.

5. Hajjar (2010) provides the basis for this cross-cultural competence subsection.
6. The majority of the documents focused on post-9/11 advising cases and yielded a final set of twenty applicable documents, but another group (fifteen documents) provided a relevant historical context of the US advising mission.
7. The findings about the importance of subjectivity in defining advisory success and the folly of overemphasizing objective or precise measures of effectiveness links to Sookermany's (2012) discussion of similar assessment processes in the contextualistperspective, which breaks with universalist notions that demand absolutes, rules, and total objectivity.
8. This analysis does not intend to overstate contractors' motivation to serve for financial profits. This study reveals generally hard-working, competent, and relevant contractor advisor team members who also worked to help counterparts gain autonomy and proficiency (Kelty and Bierman 2013). But I deduce the main motivation for most civilian contractors to serve on advisor teams, especially in combat theaters, constitutes financial motivation and perceptions of desirable compensation. Occupational orientations (e.g., financial compensation) also motivate active duty military members to serve, but this study did not uncover occupational motivations to be as strong in active duty military members as in civilian contractors.
9. Sookermany (2012) discusses how contemporary militaries transform towards a postmodern form by incorporating a constructionist perspective that includes more intricate and flexible soldier skillsets, which supports this study's argument for the rise of sophisticated cultural tools in emergent postmodern western armed forces.
10. Hajjar (2014a) elaborates on the recommended innovation of a new culture variable in postmodern military theory.

References

Abbott, Andrew D. 1998. *The System of Professions: An Essay on the Division of Expert Labor*. Chicago, IL: University of Chicago Press.

Deady, Timothy. 2009. "MiTT Advisor: A Year with the Best Division in the IRAQI ARMY." *Military Review* 89(6):43–56.

DiMaggio, Paul J. 1997. "Culture and Cognition." *Annual Review of Sociology* 23:263–287.

Ender, Morten G. 2009. *American Soldiers in Iraq: McSoldiers or Innovative Professionals?* New York: Routledge.

Etzioni, Amitai. 1961. *A Comparative Analysis of Complex Organizations: On Power, Involvement, and Their Correlates*. New York: Free Press.

French, John P. R. Jr. and Bertram Raven. 1959. "The Bases of Social Power." Pp. 150–167 in Dorwin Cartwright, ed. *Studies in Social Power*. Ann Arbor, MI: Institute for Social Research.

Geertz, Clifford J. 1973. *The Interpretation of Cultures*. New York: Basic.

Griswold, Wendy. 1994. *Cultures and Societies in a Changing World*. Thousand Oaks, CA: Pine Forge Press.

Grube, William. 2008. "The Evolution of Combined U.S. Marine Corps/Iraqi Army Operations: A Company Commander's Perspective, Fallujah, Iraq, September 2006 to April 2006." Pp. 210–223 in Donald Stoker, ed. *Military Advising and Assistance: From Mercenaries to Privatization, 1815–2007*. New York: Routledge.

Hajjar, Remi M. 2010. "A New Angle on the U.S. Military's Emphasis on Building Cross-Cultural Competence: Connecting In-Ranks' Cultural Diversity to Cross-Cultural Competence." *Armed Forces and Society* 36(2):247–263.

Hajjar, Remi M. 2014a. "Emergent Postmodern US Military Culture." *Armed Forces and Society* 40(1):118–145.

Hajjar, Remi M. 2014b. "Military Warriors as Peacekeeper-Diplomats: Building Productive Relationships with Foreign Counterparts in the Contemporary Military Advising Mission." *Armed Forces and Society* 40(4):647–672.

Hajjar, Remi M. and Morten G. Ender. 2005. "McDonaldization in the US Army: A Threat to the Profession." Pp. 515–530 in Don M. Snider and Lloyd J. Matthews, eds. *The Future of the Army Profession*. Boston, MA: McGraw Hill.

Harvey, David. 1989. *The Condition of Postmodernity: An Enquiry into the Origins of Cultural Change*. Cambridge, MA: Blackwell.

Janowitz, Morris. 1977. "From Institutional to Occupational: The Need for Conceptual Continuity." *Armed Forces and Society* 4(1):51–54.

Kelty, Ryan. 2008. "The Navy's Maiden Voyage: Effects of Integrating Sailors and Civilian Mariners on Deployment." *Armed Forces and Society* 34(4):536–564.

Kelty, Ryan and Alex Bierman. 2013. "Ambivalence on the Front Lines: Perceptions of Contractors in Iraq and Afghanistan." *Armed Forces and Society* 39(1):5–27.

Kelty, Ryan and David R. Segal. 2007. "The Civilianization of the U.S. Military: Army and Navy Case Studies of the Effects of Civilian Integration on Military Personnel." Pp. 213–239 in Thomas Jäger and Gerhard Kümmel, eds. *Private Military and Security Companies: Chances, Problems, Pitfalls, and Prospects*. Wiesbaden, Germany: VS Verlag für Sozialwissenschaften.

Miles, Jeffrey A. 2012. *Management and Organization: A Jossey-Bass Reader*. San Francisco, CA: A Jossey-Bass.

Miles, Matthew and Michael Huberman. 1994. *Qualitative Data Analysis: An Expanded Sourcebook*. Thousand Oaks, CA: Sage Publications.

Montgomery, James D. 1998. "Toward a Role-Theoretic Conception of Embeddedness." *American Journal of Sociology* 104(1):92–125.

Moskos, Charles C. and Frank R. Wood, eds. 1988. *The Military: More Than Just a Job?* Washington, DC: Pergamon-Brassey's International Defense.

Moskos, Charles C., John A. Williams, and David R. Segal, eds. 2000. *The Postmodern Military: Armed Forces after the Cold War*. New York: Oxford University Press.

Perez, Celestino Jr. 2012. "The Soldier as Lethal Warrior and Cooperative Political Agent: on the Soldier's Ethical and Political Obligations toward the Indigenous Other."*Armed Forces and Society* 38(2):177–204.

Ramsey, Robert D. III. 2006. "Advising Indigenous Forces: American Advisors in Korea, Vietnam, and El Salvador." *Global War on Terrorism Occasional Paper 18*. Fort Leavenworth, KS: Combat Studies Institute Press.

Ritzer, George. 1975. "Professionalization, Bureaucratization and Rationalization: The Views of Max Weber." *Social Forces* 53(4):627–634.

Schein, Edgar. 2010. *Organizational Culture and Leadership*. 4th ed. San Francisco, CA: Jossey-Bass.

Segal David R. and Mady W. Segal. 1983. "Change in Military Organization." *Annual Review of Sociology* 9:151–170.

Sewell, William H. 1992. "A Theory of Structure: Duality, Agency, and Transformation." *The American Journal of Sociology* 98(1):1–29.

Siebold, Guy L. 2001. "Core Issues and Theory in Military Sociology." *Journal of Political and Military Sociology* 29(Summer):140–159.

Simmons, Anna. 2013. "21st Century Culture Wars: Advantage Them." The Philadelphia Papers. Philadelphia, PA: Foreign Policy Research Institute.

Sookermany, Anders McD. 2012. "What Is a Skillful Soldier? An Epistemological Foundation for Understanding Military Skill Acquisition in (Post) Modernized Armed Forces." *Armed Forces and Society* 38(4):582–603.

Stoker, Donald, ed. 2008. *Military Advising and Assistance: From Mercenaries to Privatization, 1815–2007*. New York: Routledge Press.

Swidler, Ann. 1986. "Culture in Action: Symbols and Strategies." *American Sociological Review* 51(2):273–286.

Swidler, Ann. 2001. *Talk of Love: How Culture Matters*. Chicago, IL: University of Chicago Press.

Turner, Jonathon H. 1988. *A Theory of Social Interaction*. Stanford, CA: Stanford University Press.

United States Government U.S. Army. 2006. U.S. Military Field Manual 3–24: Counterinsurgency. Retrieved February 16, 2016 (http://fas.org/irp/doddir/army/fm3-24fd.pdf).

Williams, John A. 2008. "The Military and Society: Beyond the Postmodern Era." *Orbis* 52(2):199–216.

Winslow, Donna. 2007. "Military Organization and Culture from Three Perspectives: The Case of Army." Pp. 67–88 in Giuseppe Caforio, ed. *Social Sciences and the Military: An Interdisciplinary Overview*. London: Routledge.

Wong, Leonard. 2005. "Why Professionals Fight: Combat Motivation in the Iraq War." Pp. 491–513 in Don M. Snider and Lloyd J. Matthews, eds. *The Future of the Army Profession*. Boston, MA: McGraw-Hill.

Yukl, Gary, and Bruce J. Tracey. 1992. "Consequences of Influence Tactics used with Subordinates, Peers, and the Boss." *Journal of Applied Psychology* 77(4):525–535.

Zalmon, Amy. 2006/2007. "Waging the First Postmodern War: Inside the G.I. Cultural Awareness Program." *World Policy Journal* 23(4):35–42.

The Privatization of Civil-Security Sector Relations and the Struggle for Public Security in Iraq

Andreas Krieg
King's College London

Political and Military Sociology: An Annual Review, 2016, Vol. 44: 79–101.

This article explains the rise of insurgencies in Maliki's Iraq after 2006 through a new conceptual framework of civil-security sector relations. As will be demonstrated, the spread of ISIS across Iraq in face of a failing security sector can be attributed to a disruption of the relationship between the state's security sector and local communities—a disruption that was instigated by the former Prime Minister Maliki trying to "coup proof" his regime. He gained control over the state's security sector by tying it to him personally through sectarian, kinship, and patrimonial ties. As a consequence, the state's security forces were deprived of their ability to conduct effective counterinsurgency. Even worse, this coup-proofing policy drove away from the state those communities that felt unprotected and insecure—sentiments which were exploited by insurgency groups presenting themselves as alternative security providers. With the state unwilling and unable to provide public security inclusively, those left unprotected became recruits for alternative security providers promising to cater for communal security needs. As this article shows, the purposeful disruption of civil-security sector relations by the Maliki regime has caused the state to fail to protect particular sectarian out-groups. Ultimately, these communities have risen against the state-supporting sectarian security providers who are now competing for control in a state of anarchy.

Introduction

When the mujahedeen of the Islamic State in Iraq and al-Sham (ISIS) overran the Northern Iraqi city of Mosul in June 2014, the international community was stunned by the ineffectiveness of the numerically superior Iraqi security forces abandoning their posts. A few hundred jihadist insurgents were able to seize a city that was protected by three divisions of the Iraqi Armed Forces (IAF)—armed forces who had been trained, educated, and equipped for more than $100 billion after 2006. The post-Saddam US-led security sector reform (SSR) effort was put into question by ISIS's rapid advances throughout 2014 that left indigenous Iraqi security forces outperformed, outclassed, and defeated. A link can be made between the insurgency wave on which ISIS rose to power and the disrupted bond between the Iraqi security sector and local communities.

This article develops a conceptual framework of civil-security sector relations (CSSR) that will be applied to Maliki's Iraq post-2006. In so doing, this article does not rely on conventional theory of civil-military relations, which exclusively looks at the relationship between society, state, and military through the normative prism of civilian control. Instead, it widens the focus on the relationship between those seeking security and those providing for it by looking at the security sector as a whole. In the case of Iraq this security sector has been fairly diversified. The normative virtue of civil-security sector relations in this article derives from the civilian authority's ability and willingness to inclusively translate individual security needs into public-security provision. A distinction will be made here between public and private security provision, whereby the former describes the inclusive provision of security for all individuals within the community and the latter defines security provision as an exclusive benefit for a selected group of individuals.

Prime Minister Maliki has privatized civil-security sector relations along sectarian and kinship lines. The key premise of this article is that, in so doing, he not only deprived the security sector of its ability to effectively conduct counterinsurgency but also directly fueled the insurgency by driving communities away from the government into the hands of insurgents as alternative security providers. Similar to other security sectors in the Arab world, the Iraqi security sector has developed under Maliki into a private force unable to provide public security for Iraqis inclusively. The privatization of CSSR in Iraq resulted in security being primarily provided on the basis of sectarian affiliation and loyalty, creating a significant outsider problem for those left unprotected. Thereby, in accordance with Roessler's (2001) theory of ethnic exclusion as a means of coup proofing in Africa, Maliki's attempt to protect his regime from the possible intervention of the security sector through privatization has exposed his regime to rising levels of insurgency. The reason is that among Iraqi communities feeling marginalized or even threatened by an increasingly privatized security sector, the readiness grew to support alternative nonstatutory security providers such as ISIS.

The first part of the article will introduce the conceptual framework and illustrate the traditional nature of CSSR in the Arab world. It continues by explaining the mechanisms employed by the Maliki regime to privatize civil-security sector relations and analyzing the effects on the relationship among society, state, and security sector. It concludes by causally linking public sentiments of insecurity with the rise of alternative security providers on the local and transnational levels, of which ISIS is the most prominent.

The Public/Private Nature of Civil-Security Sector Relations (CSSR)

Traditionally the relationship between those providing security and those benefitting from it has been conceptualized under the umbrella of "civil-military relations" (CMR). CMR describes the relationship between the civilian and the military sphere and is ultimately linked to the sociopolitical dimension of the social contract. While different accounts of the social contract exist, some more liberal than others, at the heart of all conceptualizations of this sociopolitical agreement is the factor of security. Whether from the perspective of Hobbes, Locke, or Rousseau, the social contract is a security arrangement between an authority or sovereign and a community of individuals, whereby the former agrees to provide public security inclusively for all individuals within this community. This aspect of the inclusivity of security is thereby most pronounced in the liberal accounts of Locke or Rousseau. Looking at Iraq as a typical case of CMR in the Arab world, this article more adequately refers to the social contract in more authoritarian or even coercive terms—as in the accounts of Hobbes (2004) and Carl Schmitt. Here, the sovereign of the primary societal provider of security is somewhat external to the community he protects. That is to say, while the sovereign receives his legitimacy from being able to protect the community from external and internal threats, he cannot be formally held accountable by the community as the social contract here is not the direct product of a general societal will (Schmitt 2005, 2007). Both in authoritarian and liberal sociopolitical affairs, the sovereign has to raise a security sector to live up to its social contractarian obligation to provide security for the community. What consequently emerges is the Clausewitzian trinity of society, sovereign, and soldier, which not just in normative liberal theory ought to revolve around the society's inclusive security (Clausewitz 1832). The security relationship between the sovereign and his agents is what has been coined civil-military relations. While in the Western world the term civil-military relations adequately describes the relationship between society, state, and the primary security provider, in the Arab world the relationship between security providers and benefactors is far more complex—a diversified security sector protects a heterogeneous society. When examining the Arab world, one has to consider the entire spectrum of the security sector including the military, the constabulary, paramilitary as well as intelligence organizations—all of which have overlapping security roles internally as well as externally. Consequently, this article will expand the focus from narrow civil-military to civil-security sector relations (CSSR) when looking at Iraq.

Linked to democratic governance, in the theories of Huntington (2003) and Janowitz (1960), civil-military relations have traditionally been about how to ensure that the military is powerful enough to ensure the security of society and state while at the same time not intervening in the civilian sociopolitical sphere to further its own corporate military interests at the expense of its sovereign. Hence, CMR has been understood as the civilian control over the military, ensuring that the latter obediently serves the interests of the sociopolitical union of society and state without involving itself in the civilian sphere. Thereby, these conventional approaches to CMR are a product of Western liberal thought and are rooted in a liberal approach to the social contract—that is, are founded on the normative notion of the primacy of society over the state and security sector.

As mentioned above, sociopolitical affairs in the Arab world are not liberal in nature but instead display typical characteristics of authoritarian regimes in the developing world. Governance complexes in the Arab world widely fail to do justice to the liberal social contractarian idea of the primacy of society as the principal over sociopolitical and security affairs. In the Arab world, civilian control over the security sector is not a virtue in itself in absence of liberal democratic governance. As the relationship between sovereign and society in the Arab world tends to be authoritarian and often coercive in nature, civilian control of the security sector does not extend to the people's control but instead is limited to regime control.

As Svolik argues, authoritarian sovereigns are trapped between two interrelated issues: first, authoritarian control; and second, authoritarian power sharing (2012: 2). The first problem relates to controlling the people—more often than not excluded from the benefits of security provided by the regime. The second problem relates to sharing power with those elites and forces that provide the sovereign with this authoritarian control of the people. Thereby, civilian control of the security sector in the Arab world often refers to the extent to which the regime is able to corrupt the security sector to coerce society.

Hence, in the Arab world the effectiveness of the relationship between those providing security and society seeking protection should be much more defined on the basis of the inherent normative ambition of the social contract: to bring into existence a sovereign and a security apparatus able to provide security inclusively for society at large. The inclusivity of security that sovereign and security agents are able and willing to provide seems to be a more credible criterion to assess the effectiveness of civil-security sector relations. To that extent this article takes an outcome-oriented approach to CSSR, judging this security relationship based on its inherent social contractarian raison d'être. That is to say, the healthier the relationship between those supposed to benefit from security, namely society, and those providing for it, the security sector, the more the latter will be willing to provide for the security needs of the former inclusively. Here, the article suggests a distinction of public and private civil-security sector relations.

Conceptually the terms public and private can be traced back to the Ancient Greek dichotomy between the *oikos*, meaning "house" or "household," and the *polis*, namely the polity (Roy 1999: 1). Etymologically, the terms public and private are derivatives of the Latin *poplicus*, meaning "of the people," and *privatus*, meaning "withdrawn from public life." What does that mean for the differences in civil-security sector relations?

Public civil-security sector relations are the ideal type of relations founded on a close relationship between the security provider and the public triggering the former to provide security as a public good for all individuals in society inclusively. Private civil-security sector relations, on the contrary, are relations between society and security provider that are disrupted by either the security provider itself or the state. Private civil-security sector relations are characterized by exclusivity whereby the security sector is disconnected from society to allow security providers to provide security as an exclusive private good.[1] Hence, in the Arab world where regimes have traditionally viewed society not as the principal beneficiary of security but as a potential source of regime insecurity, regimes have invested into the privatization of civil-security sector relations by tying the security sector not to the inclusive public-security interests of society but to the private security interests of the regime.

Traditional Civil-Security Sector Relations in the Arab World

Similar to other parts of the developing world, governance in the Arab world has traditionally been an exclusive affair whereby authoritarian sovereigns rarely advance public-security interests but instead serve private interests of exclusive patrimonial or patronage networks. It is not so much the autocratic style of governance that undermines the social contractarian bond between society and sovereign as much as it is the aspect of exclusivity with which the sovereign renders services to society. Roessler describes a similar phenomenon in Africa, whereby authoritarian regimes attempt to minimize the competition for power in multiethnic states by ethnic exclusion, leaving a great part of society either on the fringes or outside the ranks of regime protégés (2011: 302). The consequence of exclusive governance is societal marginalization and widespread sentiments of public insecurity—sentiments that can prompt dissent and revolt. While not all Arab states are multiethnic, exclusive governance based on sectarian, religious, ethnic, ideological, political, or socioeconomic fault lines is widespread—a reality that has arguably been a key driver of the so-called Arab Spring.

Confronted with simmering dissent, the main challenge for regimes in the Arab world is an aggravation of the intrinsic dilemma of civil-security sector relations: how to create a coercive security apparatus powerful enough to protect the private interests of the regime against public dissidence while ensuring that the security sector does not turn against the regime itself (2012). In the Arab world regimes have invested highly into privatizing security sectors, namely disrupting the ties between society and security sector and realigning the security sector's raison d'être with the private security interests of the regime.

The privatization of civil-security sector relations is an effort at "coup-proofing" aiming at increasing the security sector's costs for mutiny by decreasing its benefits (Quinlivan 1999). Privatizing or depublicizing CSSR has become the means for Arab regimes to establish control over those holding both the capability and the legitimate right to use force. Five means can be identified that to a varying degree have been employed by Arab regimes to retain personal and private control over the statutory security sector: first, the diversification of the security sector; second, the centralization of command structures; third, the constant rotation of stakeholders; fourth, "commissarism;" and fifth, favoritism. These five means can be broadly divided into three categories of structural, coercive, and accommodative means of privatizing CSSR—all of which enhance the control of the regime at the expense of the security sector's bonds with the public.

The diversification of the security sector has been the most prominent structural means of privatization by Arab regimes trying to challenge the "corporateness" of security providers. A unitary security sector revolving around merely the armed forces and the constabulary carries the risk that few security providers achieve a high degree of organizational "corporateness," thereby making it difficult for both society and state to exercise control over these security providers. Perlmutter's concept of the praetorian army (1969), namely a deep state (Freely 2007) or *imperium in imperio* (state within the state), constitutes a threat for liberal and authoritarian regimes alike. The reason is that the "corporateness" of a praetorian security provider could create a power base around a group of armed individuals whose esprit de corps might be opposed to serving both society and state. For the regimes of the Arab world, a high degree of "corporateness" does not only mean the loss of control over the security provider but potentially the formation of a counter pole to the regime that might align with the public. Thus, the diversification of the security sector by creating parallel security providers with overlapping security functions stirs competition, keeps corporate security providers in check, and creates private security providers that are bound to the regime through bonds of kinship, party loyalties, or financial incentives (Brooks 2008: 37). These parallel security providers, or dual militaries, enhance the loyalties of the security sector to the regime while increasing the costs of cooperating with potential dissidents in the public (Quinlivan 1999: 141). The spectrum of parallel security providers includes numerically superior constabulary forces in Egypt, the Republican Guard in Saddam's Iraq, and extraconstitutional unconventional security providers such as the *Shabiha* militias in Syria.

Arab regimes also invest in the centralization of command structures by monopolizing command authority on the strategic level with little delegation to decision makers on the operational or tactical level. Thereby, regimes undermine the "corporateness" of security providers, deprive individual commanders of influence and authority while allowing the regime to micromanage operational and tactical decisions (Pollack 2002: 429). Key command posts, although filled with regime loyalists, are subject to constant rotation, further undermining potential alternative power bases in the security sector.

"Commissarism" is a frequently used coercive means by Arab regimes to disrupt public relations between the security sector and society. Based on the Soviet model of commissars monitoring the esprit de corps, sentiments, and motivations of soldiers and officers in the armed forces, this has produced a tight regime of monitoring and intimidation by internal security services. Either bound to the regime through ties of kinship and ethnic affiliation or by party membership and ideology, competing military intelligence services operate on the tactical, operational, and strategic levels to ensure the commitment of security providers to regime security (Brooks 2008: 41).

The most common means of privatizing civil-security sector relations in the Arab world has been accommodation through different forms of favoritism. Sectarian or kinship-based favoritism is a means to tie the security sector into the extensive patronage network of the regime. Thereby, favoritism allows the regime to merge the private interests of the elites with the corporate interests of the security sector. Consequently, the survival of the regime becomes synonymous with the maintenance of the security provider's status in terms of power and commercial business opportunities (Bellin 2012: 132). Key positions in the security sector are filled with individual protégés of the regime whose personal ties to the authoritarian leader ensure individual loyalties that are further forged by the transaction of loyalty for benefits or allegiance for status (Baram 1997; Pollack 2002; Philips 2011; Cavatorta and Durac 2011). While kinship-based favoritism only works on a smaller scale for key positions, sectarian favoritism allows entire security providers to recruit individuals who are tied to the regime by sectarian bonds. As such, sectarian favoritism is an effective means of undermining the relationship between large parts of society and the security sector that accepts other sectarian groups more readily as communal outsiders.

Regimes have also allowed security providers to become profiteers through a form of economic favoritism. Regimes have granted security providers privileged access to the market in an effort to build patrimonial bonds between the regime and those under arms. While regular transactions such as commissions from procurement budgets, salaries, and allowances are the preferred way to literally buy the security provider's loyalty, irregular transactions refer to the regime's granting of exclusive access to legal and illegal business opportunities in the defence and civilian industry (Bill and Springborg 2000: 192). As the security sector becomes increasingly involved in generating profits through various economic activities, rent-seeking behavior takes precedence over serving public-security interests. At the same time, with rent seeking becoming a priority, loyalty to the regime becomes tied to the security sector's privilege to continue to extract rents from the established patrimonial fiefdoms.

Civil-Security Sector Relations in Maliki's Iraq

The fall of the Saddam regime in 2003 brought with it the collapse of one of the most personalized and privatized governance systems in the world. In many ways Saddam's Iraq had been representative of sociopolitical and civil-security sector relations in the Arab world. In 2003, the United States had the unique opportunity to redesign both Iraq's governance system and its security sector. Haunted by the shadow of Saddam and his Baath Party, the Coalition Provisional Authority (CPA) installed by the United States to administer Iraq's transition tried to eradicate any traces of Saddam's Baathist regime. In the context of already rising sectarian tensions, the CPA initiated a radical de-Baathification program affecting the administration and the security sector. Practically overnight more than 300,000 mostly Sunni Baath Party members were excluded from participating in the building of a new sociopolitical system (Brigham 2014: 161–162). In an effort to prevent the country from sliding into complete anarchy, the CPA delegated authority to those who had little or no affiliation with the old Baathist regime—many from Shia circles in the South or from those returning from exile. In the security sector, the main focus was on building capacity quickly amid ongoing sectarian tensions, often disregarding the particular sociohistorical legacy of the various ethnic communities in Iraq (Slocombe 2004: 1).

The de-Baathification program fuelled sectarian tensions that erupted as Saddam's coercive security sector disintegrated. Decades of victimization and marginalization had created, particularly among the country's Shias, a security paranoia, which prompted the creation of vigilante and militia groups in the light of rising insecurity. In fear of marginalization and Shia reprisal, Sunnis responded by setting up their own militia groups—a process that was aided by an extensive release of Baathists into the community. As a consequence, the state building and security sector initiatives of the CPA were already placed into a malignant environment filled with resentment and armed opposition. The interim government that was put in place under the direction of the CPA quickly extended bonds of patronage into communities and militia groups on the ground.

By the time Nouri al-Maliki came into power in 2006, the overall security context had been shaped already by exclusiveness, marginalization, and distrust. Baghdad had already evolved into a Shia power base, where Sunnis were overwhelmed by the power struggle between rival Shia blocs (Tripp 2007: 277). Under Maliki the authoritarian nature of the Iraqi governance complex that already had emerged under his predecessors took further shape. De-Baathification developed into de facto de-Sunnification. Eager to restore security in Iraq, the US turned a blind eye to Maliki's increasingly authoritarian leadership even as the fragile state of security came at the expense of political and sectarian opponents. Concerns that Maliki's Iraq more and more drifted into a dictatorial fierce state fell on deaf ears in the United States as Washington was preoccupied with a swift disengagement that required both a state of security as well as the capacity to uphold it (Damon and Tawfeeq 2011).

More importantly, Maliki's Iraq had become a sectarian order, where for the first time in Iraq's history, Sunnis were radically marginalized (Kirmanj 2013: 194). The collapse of Saddam's old order had provided the vacuum for a sectarian power struggle between and within communities. In the fragile security environment of Iraq in 2006, Maliki saw his regime primarily threatened by Shia infighting between the Sadrist militia men and the Badr Corps—the former, an Iranian surrogate militia with loyalties to Maliki. The prime minister tried to position himself as the undisputed leader of the Shia bloc, thereby having to galvanize Shia identity vis-à-vis Iraq's Sunni community as the outsider (Rayburn 2014). Deliberately portraying Sunni dissidence as the attempt of the old regime to regain power in Iraq, Maliki played on existing sectarian tensions to crack down on former Baathists—an excuse to purge Sunnis from the security sector and administration. Maliki's attempt to consolidate power was built on the back of identity politics and a regime-instilled "sectarianization" of both politics and security provision. In accordance with Posen's concept of the security dilemma in ethnic conflict, Maliki exploited the decades-old security paranoia of Shia communities to make matters of security an exclusively private in-group rather than inclusively public affair (Posen 1993).

Confronted with a simmering insurgency particularly in Sunni areas, Maliki did not only have to consolidate his power over Shia blocs but also over the security sector that he was eager to transform into a private tool for regime security. Despite the fact that the United States had invested more than $100 billion into security sector reform in Iraq since 2006 alone, the United States' ambitions of creating an effective public-security sector were undermined by the deteriorating security situation. Regime resilience amid insurgency and acts of terrorism had taken precedence over providing public security for Iraqis inclusively (Krieg 2014). As a typical military dictator, Maliki assigned great importance to security sector loyalty as the center of gravity for regime resilience (Acemoglu 2010). Consequently, the regime invested in privatizing the relationship between the security sector and society.

The key means of privatizing civil-security sector relations under Maliki was sectarian and kinship-based favoritism. Key military positions on the strategic and operational level were staffed with loyal companions and *Malikiyoun*, a kinship-based group of trustees (Rayburn 2012). Particularly among the generals, Maliki used the American de-Baathification excuse to oust individuals from central command positions. Empty seats were filled with Maliki loyalists, many of whom were Shiites with links to Iran. In 2013, eleven out of fourteen Iraqi Army division commanders were Shiites, many with biographies similar to Maliki's (Sullivan 2013: 18). Here, personal and sectarian loyalties were more important than merit or operational effectiveness. Among Sunni communities, these privatization practises led to feelings of alienation as the perception became common that the security sector was undergoing a wider "Shiaization" policy to create a private sectarian force.

The division between society and the security sector was intensified by structural means of privatization. Similar to other ministerial portfolios, Maliki tried to circumvent formal institutional checks and balances by erecting an extraconstitutional infrastructure allowing him to be the commander in chief to circumvent decisions from the Ministry of Interior and Ministry of Defence (Al-Ali 2014). The Office of the Commander in Chief (OCINC), a new shadow institution staffed with loyalists, was used by Maliki to personally micromanage operational decisions bypassing the chain of command on the strategic level (Sullivan 2013: 11). Further, Maliki incited institutional competition. Six intelligence agencies were set up in parallel providing identical services allowing the patron to play one against the other in a game of divide and rule. The US-sponsored Iraqi National Intelligence Service (INIS) was countered with the Ministry of State for National Security Affairs (MSNSA) (Sullivan 2013: 15). The latter was taken over in 2009 by a member of the *Malikiyoun*, Falah Fayadh, who consequently transformed the organization into a commissarist tool for the Maliki patronage to eliminate political opponents (Rayburn 2014: 60).

Moreover, Maliki tried to diversify the security sector by increasingly relying on non-statutory security providers—namely Shia militias—to act as progovernment force multipliers for counterterrorist operations (Carey et al. 2012). Some militias had already been integrated into the Ministry of Interior's (MoI) structure prior to Maliki's appointment. Others were officially given amnesty to operate death squads against anyone the regime considered to be Baathist—a label awarded arbitrarily to former Sunni members of Saddam's administration (Carey et al. 2012: 79). The Badr Corps often conducted joint operations with the MoI while Shia death squads loyal to extremist cleric Muqtada al-Sadr were allowed to continue their policy of ethnic cleansing of Baghdad's Sunni neighbourhoods with impunity. Calls by the international community to actively clamp down on the death squads were ignored by Maliki, who benefitted from repression of potential Sunni or Baathist opponents (Woodward 2012, chapter 9).

In addition, Maliki increasingly tied selected military divisions to him personally. Units of the Iraqi Army's Sixth Division stationed in Baghdad were staffed with *Malikiyoun* on the strategic level and with Shia servicemen close to Maliki's Islamic Dawa Party on the operational and tactical level. They were entrusted with the security of the Green Zone and personal security of Maliki. Under the personal command of Maliki's son Ahmed, the Baghdad Brigade, as a subunit of the Sixth Division, developed into a quasi-praetorian guard for the regime (Rayburn 2014: 57). In reference to the *"Fedayeen Saddam,"* Saddam's personal guard controlled by his son Udai, Maliki's praetorian guard earned the title *"Fedayeen Maliki."* More importantly, Maliki took control of the Iraqi Special Operations Force (ISOF), a special force of a few thousand capable and well-equipped men trained by the United States. Initially operating exclusively with the authority of a ministerial decree, the ISOF has subsequently developed into a shadow force under direct authority of the OCINC. In this way, the ISOF operates as a private extraconstitutional force under the direct control of the prime minister. Instead of acting as the public's counterterrorism force, the ISOF has been effectively abused to contain dissidents, serving as the regime's private security provider (Bauer 2009).

Moreover, Maliki has further transformed an already profiteering security sector into patrimonial networks. Key protégées of Maliki's patronage were allowed to abuse security providers and units as personal

fiefdoms for self-enrichment. Funds distributed by the patron were chan-
nelled to hollow units mostly staffed with ghost soldiers whose salary
and allowances enriched the commanders—a circumstance that allowed
Maliki to literally buy loyalty (Parker and Ryan 2014). An International
Crisis Group (ICG) report from 2010 quotes an Australian military officer
involved in security sector reform, stating that:

> Cronyism, bribery, kickbacks, extortion, and even the threat and use of physical
> intimidation and violence within the [Iraqi security forces are] commonplace and
> [are] getting worse. Commanders are not chosen for their ability, but rather based on
> whether or not they have paid the Division Commander the fee he demands. Falsifica-
> tion of patrol reports, theft of government supplies for sale on the black market, and
> imprisonment of anyone who stands up to such crimes essentially crushes individual
> initiative and any desire to do the right thing (2010: 30).

Through structural means of privatization, favoritism, and profiteering, Maliki transformed the Iraqi security sector into a private sectarian
tool of the regime. By co-opting and tying the security sector to him
through private loyalties, Maliki has been able to contain threats to his
authoritarian rule from the elites. Those elites with the coercive power
to suppress opponents of the regime had become key protégés of Maliki
tied to him through commercial interests, bonds of kinship, and sectarian affiliation. While these privatization practices might have reduced
the risks of an armed coup against the regime, they have severely
increased the vulnerability of the entire country to the dynamics of
insurgency. Roessler explains this trade-off between coup proofing and
effective counterinsurgency as a result of ethnic exclusion practises in
Africa (2011). The case of Iraq demonstrates that it was not only ethnic
exclusion that increased insurgent activity and dissidence but also the
privatization of the security sector through profiteering, kinship-based
favoritism, and "commissarism" that undermined its ability and willingness to respond to public-security demands. Even worse, the Iraqi
security sector became a private tool of repression, intimidation, and
coercion, increasing sentiments of marginalization and disenfranchise-
ment particularly among Sunni communities.

   Among those marginalized communities subjected to ethnic cleansing, arbitrary detention, torture, killing, and disappearances (Department
of State 2011), the alienation from the Baghdad regime led to rebellion
and insurgency that was further fuelled by those former Baathist elites
purged from the administration. As Maliki presented the overall security situation in the country as improving toward the end of the 2000s,
many observers turned a blind eye to simmering insurgency activity in

the predominantly Sunni areas of Western and Northern Iraq. The rise of insurgency in Iraq can be explained with Roessler's observation that

> exclusive practices facilitate insurgency formation in several ways. Purges and defections generate a pool of disaffected elites who can serve as dissident entrepreneurs and use their experience and skills to raise the political consciousness among the excluded group, set a revolutionary agenda, and help to organize a rebel group (2011: 314).

The Rise of Alternative Security Providers

Following the appointment of Maliki as the prime minister, the already fragile social contract that the coalition had put in place continued to crumble further. The gap between in-groups and out-groups, namely those communities protected by the regime versus those communities excluded, widened further. Security in Iraq—as elusive as it was by the end of the 2000s, as Al Qaeda had been defeated by a coalition of Sunni tribes enfranchised by the coalition military—has become effectively a private good. The regime primarily catered for the security needs of the *Malikiyoun* and affiliated Shia communities and secondly for the wider Shia communities of Iraq. Sunni Arab, Kurdish, and minority communities were largely left unprotected. As Posen observes, with the collapse of inclusive public security, groups feeling unprotected have to provide for what the sovereign is supposed to provide: security. However, lacking the attributes of states these outgroups are forced to provide security as a private good (1993: 38). The same can be said for Iraq post-2006.

Large parts of Iraqi society had lost their trust in the ability or willingness of the Maliki regime to live up to its social contractarian duty of providing public security inclusively. Bonds between the privatized security sector and local communities, particularly in Sunni areas, were virtually nonexistent. As a consequence, amid this widespread public sentiment of insecurity among those communities suffering under the repression of the increasingly sectarian security forces, militias and insurgency groups promising inclusive security for these marginalized communities had little difficulty building a social base. Looking at the Iraqi security sector as an external actor providing security for the regime and its key protégés rather than communal interests, marginalized communities were seeking protection. Public dissidence spread beyond Sunni Islamist, jihadist, or Baathist circles to ordinary Iraqis who were willing to support anyone promising to fill the void left by an increasingly authoritarian regime and its privatized security sector (Rayburn 2014: 238).

This was the context in which particularly the so-called Islamic State (ISIS) rose to power—an organization that in the Syrian and Iraqi context has to be considered an insurgency group. ISIS and its predecessor Islamic State in Iraq (ISI) were able to position themselves as protectors of the Sunnis (Hassan and Weiss 2015: 108), providing a sociopolitical narrative that would gradually develop into a powerful counternarrative to the failed American project of building an inclusive governance system in Baghdad (Lister 2014: 18). The ideology of the Islamic State, which was an evolution from the global jihadist agenda of Al Qaeda, envisaged an insurgent approach, namely holding and administering territory. Thereby, terror was now just a means to change existing sociopolitical authority structures (Lister 2014: 9)

This article does not try to explain the rise of ISIS solely by the disruption of civil-security sector relations in Iraq or with the privatization of security there. However, although the rise of ISIS into a powerful transnational insurgency movement was aided by the Syrian civil war, the roots and the core of the Islamic State evolved from the disenfranchised and marginalized Sunni communities in Iraq—namely those outsider communities who had been left unprotected by the Maliki regime and its privatized security sector. It was the merger between Saddam's former Baathist elites, who had been infiltrating jihadist circles already throughout the 1990s, and jihadist insurgents in American custody that laid the foundation of the Islamic State in Iraq after 2006. Both saw Maliki's sectarian regime as the key enemy; both saw Sunni Islam as a powerful counternarrative to the establishment in Baghdad (Hassan and Weiss 2015: 86). Here, the same dynamics were at play as Roessler identifies in African dictatorships: the excluded elites built their own power bases, set out a revolutionary agenda, and sought followers among marginalized Sunni communities (2011: 314). The terror of Maliki's privatized security sector increased the numbers of those desperate to find empowerment. Finally, even those Sunni tribes from Iraq's Western Anbar that had assisted the US-led awakening against Al Qaeda in 2006 felt increasingly powerless against the appeal of ISI as the Maliki government failed to enfranchise these tribes once Al Qaeda had disappeared.[2] While Al Qaeda tried to wage a global jihad against "Western crusaders" relying mostly on foreign mujahedeen, ISI more directly targeted the sources of sociopolitical grievances of Sunnis in Iraq. Within a state of insecurity, ISI, and later ISIS, was able to infiltrate the social fabric of Iraq's western and northern provinces. Offering to mediate in tribal feuds, co-opting young tribal leaders, and offering civilians a tightly run quasi-state infrastructure in the shadow of Maliki's "sectarianization" policies, allowed the organization since 2007 to become the alternative security provider for many Sunni Iraqis (Hassan and Weiss 2015: 133). As Hassan and Weiss write on the basis of their extensive interviews with Islamic State residents, ISIS presented itself as

> the only armed group capable of striking against the "anti-Sunni" regimes and militias in Syria, Iraq, and beyond. . . . [P]ragmatists support the group because it is effective . . . ISIS has established a semblance of order in these "governed" territories, and people view the alternatives . . . as far worse. For those weary of years of civil war, the ability to live without crime and lawlessness trumps whatever draconian rules ISIS has put into place (2015: 108).

As a consequence, those haunted by sentiments of public insecurity and victimhood have become the pragmatist appendix constituting the silent majority of the Islamic State: Sunni communities that have been allowed to govern themselves with little oversight from the radical core of the organization but with the confidence that the organization provides security. The fact that millions of Iraqi Sunnis have remained within the territory of what has become the Islamic State after its seizure of Mosul in 2014 shows that many pragmatically consider ISIS the lesser of two evils.[3] The fall of Mosul already exemplified how powerful ISIS' narrative was. The organization's reputation to cater to the Sunni communities' fundamental security needs had functioned as the Islamic State's most powerful force multiplier against a security sector that for years had failed to provide public security.

When ISIS launched its attack on Mosul in June 2014—a stronghold for Sunni dissidence particularly among many former Baathists residing there—three factors sped up the victory of the mujahedeen over Iraqi security forces: first, as mentioned above, the existence of public sympathies toward ISIS (Hamid 2014); second, the absence of a genuine bond between local communities and the security sector; and third, the operational ineffectiveness of a deprofessionalized Iraqi security sector.

The 30,000 Iraqi armed forces and policemen stationed in Iraq's second city knew that they could not rely on the support of the local population. With many soldiers coming from the Shia provinces in the South, there was a general distrust toward a civilian population that had been repeatedly subjected to arbitrary harassment and detention by uniformed security forces. Many of the Shia commanders and officers were unwilling to engage ISIS on the battlefield risking their lives to protect a city and province that was majority Sunni (Nasser 2014). While Shia security forces abandoned their posts and fled to neighbouring Kurdistan, many Sunni forces with ties to the local community deserted to protect their families against potential ISIS vengeance (Ryan and Ryan 2014).

Moreover, security forces in Mosul, similar to other cities, had developed into patrimonial networks displaying profiteering behavior. Operational effectiveness and professional merit had become negligible values (International Crisis Group 2010: 30). Military and constabulary units were run as personal fiefdoms whereby salaries and allowances were paid out personally by unit commanders as a means to create dependencies between commanders and subordinates. With commanders having the ability to withhold salaries, cut allowances, and even curtail food rationing, subordinate ranks developed trustful relationships neither with superiors nor with the organization as a whole (Krieg 2014). As a result, subordinates used the public for extortion—a practise facilitated by the lack of a bond between civilian communities and security providers. Entire units had been run as shadow forces with commanders "staffing" lower ranks with "ghost soldiers" in an effort to pocket their salaries and allowances. Consequently, when faced with the onslaught of ISIS as a highly flexible, well-coordinated force with strong morale and bonds to local tribes, many military and constabulary units in Iraq decided to desert, not trusting their own, their commander's, or the organization's capabilities and ethos.

ISIS's rapid territorial gains since 2014 have put additional strain on the already tense civil-security sector relations in the country. While some Sunni communities chose to cooperate with ISIS, other communities, mostly non-Arab and non-Sunni communities, perceive ISIS as an existential threat against which the Iraqi state ought to protect them—but often fails to do so. The rise of ISIS can be attributed to the failure of a privatized security sector to provide security inclusively as a public good. It has created a situation in which the Islamic State as a challenger to the Baghdad regime has appeared as an alternative security provider providing security exclusively as a private good to selected communities, thereby exacerbating the outsider problem. Among minorities in Iraq's northern and western provinces, dissidence has been on the rise as the mistrust in the capabilities and intentions of the security sector have triggered a mentality of self-help. Shia communities aloof to the Maliki regime, Kurds, and minority groups have adopted a sectarian rhetoric and response against ISIS, which has been perceived as primarily a Sunni Arab peril. In line with Posen's argument, these communities have relied on their own local security providers to provide security as a private good for the in-group (Posen 1993: 30). The security dilemma of this sectarian society manifests itself in a spiral of violence. The Islamic State, borne by a Sunni insurgency, has created an outsider problem for other communities in Iraq that feel threatened not just by the rise of ISIS but also by the incapability of the Iraqi security sector to protect them from ISIS. Essentially, the inability of the Iraqi state to provide for public security inclusively has undermined its very social contractarian raison d'être and has increased the pace of its sociopolitical disintegration.

Shia communities have relied more heavily on their own militias and vigilante groups to augment the capacity of widely ineffective and distrusted Iraqi security services. The regime in Baghdad has relied on the Mahdi Army, the Badr Corps, and other nonstatutory security providers to protect communities against ISIS. However, again, security has been provided as a private good. The reason is that the relationship between these security providers and local communities is exclusively based on sectarian bonds—it is locals joining local security outfits to provide local security (Fahim 2015). Sectarian outgroups have often not been protected; even worse, allegations have been raised that these Shia militia and vigilante groups have committed atrocities in retaliation against Sunnis accused of cooperating with ISIS (Fahim 2015).

In Iraq's northern provinces, Kurdish Peshmerga forces have carried the operational burden against ISIS—providing security for Kurds not just in the area under the control of the Kurdistan Regional Government (KRG) but also in Kurdish majority areas in other provinces. Peshmerga fighters of all ranks take pride in their role as inclusive protectors of Kurdistan providing shelter for all minorities—a claim that is challenged by Yezidi and Assyrian Christian minorities. While Kurds are historically united in their distrust against Arab regimes in Baghdad, minority groups living under Kurdish rule repeatedly stress that the Peshmerga do not fight as fiercely and committedly for the security of non-Muslim minorities.[4] Thus, while civil-security sector relations between Kurdish Muslim communities and Peshmerga fighters have traditionally been strong, minority groups appeared to have been disillusioned by the performance of Peshmergas in the fight for Yezidi or Assyrian areas.

Yezidi and Assyrian villagers have raised their own militias who provide security on the local level. Many minority villages in northern Kurdistan have set up check points and road blocks manned by local villagers in combat fatigues and equipped with assault rifles. Assyrian and Yezidi militias unite in distrust of the Peshmerga forces in charge of the defence of Kurdistan. The Peshmerga's initial poor performance against ISIS forces on Mount Sinjar in August 2014 led many minorities to believe that their communal fight for survival will have to be borne by the community itself in a bottom-up approach[5]—a perception that might change after the recapture of Sinjar by Peshmerga forces in November 2015 (Coles 2015).

The consequence of the absence of inclusive public security beyond the local level is the sociopolitical disintegration of Iraq affecting individual senses of belonging, identity, and social cohesion. The bottom-up provision of public security on the local level seems to foster the relationship between those providing security and its benefactors but at the same time further erodes the relationship between individuals and the statutory security sector. The social contract has been redefined, causing those excluded from the ranks of the regime to find alternative means of security provision, thereby accelerating the process of state failure. The attempt to privatize the security sector has not only failed to strengthen the regime's control over power but more importantly has also exposed the regime to a state of insurgency.

Conclusion

Similar to other authoritarian dictatorships in the developing world, Arab regimes have traditionally invested into the consolidation of domestic power through forms of exclusion or privatization. Dissidence against privatization practices are met with coercion and repression by those in power. Consequently, regimes and their key protégés have to rely primarily on the unconditional loyalty of the security sector in order to contain those who are deemed a threat to regime security. Therefore, regimes have tried to gain control over those holding arms. What has been coined coup proofing is the security sector's divorce from the public and the tying of security providers to the patronage of the regime—essentially the privatization or depublicization of civil-security sector relations.

In the literature, this privatization of the security sector, and thereby the disruption of its bond to the public, has been identified as a major obstacle to military effectiveness, namely to the security sector's ability to perform well in conventional operations (Biddle and Zirkle 1996; Pollack 2002; Pilster and Boehmelt 2011). Yet, the literature has not effectively identified how coup proofing or privatization practices affect civil-security sector relations and thereby the statutory security providers relations to the public. It is this relationship, however, that is key in effective counterinsurgency—arguably a far more important security task of security sectors today than conventional warfare.

This article has shown that in line with Roessler's theory about the trade-off between coup proofing and insurgency in Africa, the privatization of the relationship between security providers and the public on the basis of sectarian affiliation or kinship bonds significantly increases the risks of many in the Arab world. In many of the multiethnic states of the Arab world, the failure of regimes to live up to the social contractarian demand of providing public security inclusively has led to widespread rebellion and insurgency after the Arab Spring. The case of Iraq under Maliki and his successor is a stark example of how the absence of a genuine bond of trust and ownership between certain civilian communities and the security sector causes communities to feel unprotected and thus to raise or support alternative security providers. Insurgent groups and rebels promising and delivering on the provision of communal security have often received communal support despite potential ideological differences. In Iraq today, rebels, vigilante groups, and insurgents have assumed the roles of alternative security providers as the state has failed to do so. The privatized security sector has disregarded its social contractarian duty to protect the public by exclusively providing private regime security. In areas that the security sector has retreated from—particularly Anbar and Nineveh Province as well as the Kurdish areas in the North East—vacuums of insecurity have been filled by security providers that, despite failing to provide public security for Iraqis, have been able to provide security for particular communities.

The rise of ISIS as the most prominent alternative security provider has contributed to widespread feelings of insecurity, in particular among non-Sunni outgroups. As Sunni tribal leaders have pledged allegiance to the Islamic State in a pragmatic step to protect their tribes from the harassment of Baghdad's privatized security sector, security paranoia among outgroups has grown. Thus, the rise of ISIS, which has to be understood primarily as a local insurgency, has not led to the integration of Iraqi communities in the face of this common enemy but rather to sectarian polarization. The societal distrust of communities toward the regime and its security sector runs deep and has provided a fertile ground for alternative sociopolitical narratives, which receive legitimacy based on their ability to provide security. It has contributed to a redefinition of the social contract in the north where security provision is no longer the prerogative of the state but a local communal affair. As socio-political affairs revolve fundamentally around the provision of security, the rise of alternative security providers has contributed to the development of sociopolitical fragmentation.

The localization of security provision has intensified sectarian dynamics and undermined communal cohesion across Iraq.

Looking toward the future of Iraq in particular, and the Arab world more widely, it is key for new regimes and governance complexes to cater to the security needs of communities inclusively. The failure of the security sector to provide security inclusively undermines the legitimacy of the state while providing legitimacy to any insurgents or rebel groups able to provide security to a social base. Stability in Iraq depends on the ability of security providers to erect a new social contract—one that some would argue ISIS has already tried to forge with followers, sympathizers, and pragmatists in those areas worst affected by insecurity post-2003. Unless these communities are provided with a viable alternative socio-political narrative and a security apparatus able to protect, the Islamic State will be able to consolidate its power in Iraq. Security sector reform founded on a federal reorganization of security forces could enhance trust and ownership of communities to security providers that would be raised and stationed locally. Such security forces would be able to provide security inclusively as a public good on the local level but with the oversight and support from a central government.

Notes

1. In reference to security, the term "private" has often been used to describe commercially provided security. In this article the term "private" merely relates to the exclusivity with which security is provided by the security sector.
2. Author's interview with Anbar tribal leaders in Istanbul, Turkey, 6 July 2015.
3. Author's interview with Col Koshow and Gen Arsalan in Makhmour Forward Operating Base Front Line, Iraq, 6 October 2014.
4. Author's Interview with Assyrian and Yezidi villagers in Dohuk Governorate, Iraq, 4 October 2014.
5. Author's interview with Assyrian and Yezidi militias in Dohuk Governorate, Iraq, 4 October 2014.

References

Acemoglu, Daron, Davide Ticchi, and Andrea Vindigni. 2010. "A Theory of Military Dictatorships." *American Economic Journal: Macroeconomics* 2(1):1–42.

Al-Ali, Zaid. 2014. "How Maliki Ruined Iraq." *Foreign Policy*, 17 July 2014.

Baram, Amatzia. 1997. "Neo-Tribalism in Iraq: Saddam Hussein's Tribal Policies 1991–96." *International Journal of Middle East Studies* 29(1):1–31.

Bellin, Eva. 2012. "Reconsidering the Robustness of Authoritarianism in the Middle East. Lessons from the Arab Spring." *Comparative Politics* 44(2):139–157.

Biddle, Stephen and Robert Zirkle. 1996. "Technology, Civil-Military Relations and Warfare in the Developing World. *Journal of Strategic Studies* 19(2):171–212.

Bill, James and Robert Springborg. 2000. *Politics in the Middle East*. New York: Addison Wesley Longman.

Brigham, Robert K. 2014. *The United States and Iraq since 1990: A Brief History with Documents*. London: Wiley Blackwell.

Brooks, Risa. 2008. "Political-Military Relations and the Stability of Arab Regimes." Adelphi Paper 324. London: Routledge.

Bauer, Shane. 2009. "Iraq's New Death Squad." *The Nation*, 3 June 2009

Carey, Sabine C., Neil J. Mitchell, and Will Lowe. 2012. "States, the Security Sector, and the Monopoly on Violence: A New Database on Pro-Government Militias." *Journal of Peace Research* 50(2):249–258.

Cavatorta, Francesco and Vincent Durac. 2011. *Civil Society and Democratization in the Arab World: The Dynamics of Activism*. London: Routledge.

Clausewitz, Carl v. 1832. *Vom Kriege*. Berlin: Ferdinand Dümmler.

Coles, Isabel. 2015. "Kurdish Forces Seize Iraq's Sinjar Town from Islamic State." *Reuters*, 13 November 2015.

Damon, Arwa and Mohammad Tawfeeq. 2011. "Iraq's Leader Becoming a New 'Dictator,' Deputy Warns." *CNN*, 13 December 2011

Department of State. 2011. *Human Rights Reports: Iraq - 2011 Country Reports on Human Rights Practices*. May 24, 2012. Washington, DC: US State Department, Bureau of Democracy, Human Rights, and Labor.

Fahim, Kareem. 2015. "Shiite Militia Drives Back Islamic State, but Divides Much of Iraq." *The New York Times*, 7 February 2015.

Freely, Maureen. 2007. "Why They Killed Hrant Dink." *Index on Censorship* 2007, 36:15–29.

Hamid, Shadi. 2014. "The Roots of the Islamic State's Appeal." *The Atlantic*, 31 October 2014.

Hassan, Hassan and Michael Weiss. 2015. "*ISIS: Inside the Army of Terror.*" New York: Regan Arts.

Hobbes, Thomas. 2004. *Leviathan*. Sioux Falls, SD: Nuvision Publications.

Huntington, Samuel P. 2003. *The Soldier and the State: The Theory and Politics of Civil Military Relations*. Cambridge, MA: Harvard University Press.

International Crisis Group. 2010. "Loose Ends: Iraq's Security Forces Between U.S. Drawdown and Withdrawal." *Middle East Report* 99, 26 October 2010.

Janowitz, Morris. 1960. *The Professional Soldier: A Social and Political Portrait*. New York: Free Press.

Kirmanj, Sherko. 2013. *Identity and Nation in Iraq*. London: Lynne Rienner.

Krieg, Andreas. 2014. "ISIS' Success in Iraq: A Testimony to Failed Security Sector Reform." *Security Sector Reform Resource Centre*, 22 July 2014.

Lister, Charles. 2014. *Profiling the Islamic State*. Doha: Brookings Institution.

Nasser, Mostafa. 2014. "Why Did the Iraqi Army Collapse in Mosul?" *Al Akhbar English*, 13 June 2014.

Parker, Ned and Missy Ryan. 2014. "Iraqi Military Breakdown Fuelled by Corruption, Politics." *Reuters*, 13 June 2014.

Perlmutter, Amos. 1969. "The Praetorian State and the Praetorian Army: Toward a Taxonomy of Civil-Military Relations in Developing Polities." *Comparative Politics* 1(3):382–404.

Philips, Sarah. 2011. *Yemen and the Politics of Permanent Crisis*. London: Routledge.

Pilster, Ulrich and Tobias Boehmelt. 2011. "Coup Proofing and Military Effectiveness in Interstate Wars, 1967–99." *Conflict Management and Peace Science* 28(4):331–350.

Pollack, Kenneth. M. 2002. *Arabs at War: Military Effectiveness, 1948–1991*. New York: Council on Foreign Relations.

Posen, Barry S. 1993. "The Security Dilemma and Ethnic Conflict." *Survival* 35(1):27–47.

Quinlivan, James T. 1999. "Coup-Proofing: Its Practice and Consequences in the Middle East." *International Security* 24(2):131–165.

Rayburn, Joel D. 2012. "Rise of the Maliki Regime." *Journal of International Security Affairs*, 22:45–54.

Rayburn, Joel D. 2014. *Iraq After America: Strongmen, Sectarians, Resistance*. Stamford, CA: Stamford University Press.

Roessler, Philip. 2011. "The Enemy Within: Personal Rule, Coups, and Civil War in Africa. *World Politics* 63(2):300–334.

Roy, J. 1999. "'Polis' and 'Oikos' in Classical Athens." *Greece & Rome* 46(1):1–18.

Schmitt, Carl. 2005. *Political Theology: Four Chapters on the Concept of Sovereignty*. Chicago: University of Chicago Press.

Schmitt, Carl. 2007. *The Concept of the Political*. Chicago: University of Chicago Press.

Slocombe, Walter. B. 2004. "Iraq's Special Challenge: Security Sector Reform 'Under Fire'." *DCAF-SSR Year Book 2004*. Geneva: Geneva Centre for the Democratic Control of Armed Forces.

Sullivan, Marisa. 2013. "Maliki's Authoritarian Regime." *Middle East Security Report* 10. Washington: Institute for the Study of War.

Svolik, Milan W. 2012. *Politics of Authoritarian Rule*. Cambridge: Cambridge University Press.

Tripp, Charles. 2007. *A History of Iraq*. Cambridge: Cambridge University Press.

Woodward, Bob. 2012. *The War Within: A Secret White House History 2006–2008*. New York: Simon & Schuster.

On Entering the Military Organization: Decivilianization, Depersonalization, Order, and Command in the Zimbabwe National Army[1]

Godfrey Maringira
University of the Western Cape

Political and Military Sociology: An Annual Review, 2016, Vol. 44: 103–124.

The military presents a typical example of an "enclosed system" that is able to achieve the impractical; it is where soldiers are "made" from civilians. Through processes of military training recruits are depersonalized and stripped of their civilian ways by the order and command of military instructors. While the processes and practices of military training are not new or peculiar to the African military, this article reveals that, on entering the military, a recruit is forced to leave behind more than the guiding civilian perceptions about self and others. The central argument is that the relationship between soldiers and the military organization is forged through discipline, punishment, and control during military training. In addition, I emphasize the idea of "total institution" and "techniques of discipline and punishment" in constructing the soldier's new persona. I explore how recruits are stripped of and voluntarily shrug off a "civilian mentality" to adopt a "military mentality." In doing so, I draw on forty-four narratives of Zimbabwean former soldiers living in exile in South Africa.

Introduction

Welcome to St. Idiot secondary school. The headmaster is Mr. Dull, where all students are stupid. The headmaster did not go to school, but he is an Instructor. For the next six months you are not going to think; rather I will think for you. I know when you want to puff, to go to the toilet, to eat, to sleep, to walk, run, and to bathe. So relax. When you are told to jump, you don't ask why, but how high! Squad! Did I make myself clear (Alpha Romeo: quoting his military instructor on the first day of military training)?

The quote above reveals what happens to recruits upon entering a military cantonment, an organization where "undignified" language by military instructors is legitimated. The military is often portrayed as an institution which is "total" in itself. It is total because the activities that happen within it are confined and can only be understood by those within it. In this article, my central argument is that the relationship between soldiers and the military organization is forged through the punishment and discipline of decivilized and depersonalized men who come from a "civilian world" to transmogrify into that of the military. In substantiating my argument I draw from Goffman's (1961) idea of "total institution" and Foucault's (1977) "techniques of discipline and punishment." In the first section I provide some background on the Zimbabwe National Army and reveal how I met former soldiers who shared their experiences about the process of military training. I then focus on the stories of these men and what it means to be trained in the military organization. The ways in which these recruits were "made" through discipline and punishment is central to this article.

The Zimbabwe National Army

The Zimbabwean army was formed at independence in 1980. The new army was a merger of the two main guerrilla armed wings—the Zimbabwe African National Liberation Army (ZANLA), the armed wing of the Zimbabwe African National Union-Patriotic Front (ZANU-PF) led by President Robert Mugabe, and the Zimbabwe People's Revolutionary Army (ZIPRA), the armed wing of the Zimbabwe African People's Union (ZAPU) led by Joshua Nkomo—and the Rhodesian forces. The integration of these forces was carried out under the supervision of the British Military Advisory and Training Team (BMATT), which assisted in the standardization and professionalization of the military (Alao 1995; Young 1997; White 2007; Jackson 2011; Tendi 2013). Despite this integration, however, distrust between ZIPRA and ZANLA guerrillas, whose personnel were dominated by different ethnic groups (the Ndebele and Shona, respectively), persisted (Alexander 1998). It was this distrust that had earlier led to desertion within the ranks of ZIPRA, whose members were persecuted by the winning political party cadres of President Robert Mugabe's ZANLA. Deserters were perceived as dissidents. Hence, the new Fifth Brigade and ZANLA comrades aligned to President Robert Mugabe party (see also Alexander 1998; White 2007) were deployed in Matabeleland area during the *Gukurahundi* massacre (meaning the first rains that wash the chaff). In this case the chaff was thought to be not only the dissidents but also the Ndebele people.

Following this event, some scholars, like Alexander (2013) and White (2007), have argued that, despite the professionalization of the new Zimbabwe army, the military has remained heavily politicized under President Robert Mugabe's regime. In the post-2000 political crisis, the military has been linked to the perpetration of violence against supporters of the Movement of Democratic Change (MDC-T) led by Morgan Tsvangirai. However, what is not as well known is that, in seeking to serve the regime of President Robert Mugabe, soldiers without a background in the liberation struggle also became victims of prejudice in the military barracks. These soldiers, whose voices are presented in this article, view the Zimbabwe army as politicised, mainly because they were perceived as sympathizers and supporters of the MDC-T. That is, army generals and high-ranking commanders with a liberation history viewed the new generation of soldiers as a threat to the military's traditional links to the liberation struggle, a history which Ranger (2004) presents as a "patriotic history" and "Mugabe-ism"—that is, the celebration of President Robert Mugabe as the "Alpha and Omega" of Zimbabwe's history (Tendi 2008). Because the majority of soldiers without a liberation history viewed themselves as professionals, they were no longer able to serve in a politicised army that labelled them as loyalists of the opposition political party. Thus, they decided to desert and migrate to neighboring countries such as Mozambique, Botswana, and South Africa.

In Conversation with Former Soldiers

It is important for the reader to understand that I was a soldier for more than ten years in the Zimbabwe National Army, both during times of war as well as peace. I therefore understand the rationale of the stories told by these former soldiers. The motivation for this research began when I met a former comrade (pseudonym Charlie Mike) at the main Johannesburg bus station in 2009. Overjoyed to meet each other away from the army barracks, Charlie Mike used our past military drill language to greet me: "Squad chaaa!" (Attention!). I responded, "Still!" (a common and humorous response among members of the same rank).

My response conveyed that, having been commanded by a person of rank equal to mine, I was not prepared to stand at attention. It was a humorous display of nostalgia for the military past we had shared in the barracks during and after our military training. Charlie Mike and I reminisced about what we used to do, our time during military training, and what we went through in war and in the Zimbabwe army barracks. I asked Charlie Mike whether there were other former soldiers in South Africa. He was quite surprised that I was not aware of the many former soldiers in and around Johannesburg, the majority of whom had trained together. Charlie Mike shared with me the cell phone numbers of six former comrades. On parting ways, I quickly phoned them, and they were all happy to hear that I was also in the city. Each of these soldiers gave me the cell phone numbers of other former compatriots. I phoned the others, and we all agreed to meet at a restaurant in Johannesburg.

The following weekend sixteen of us met; the majority were former soldiers who had trained together as recruits and a few others who had later worked with us during our deployment in the Democratic Republic of Congo (DRC) from 1998 to 2002. My observation of these former soldiers confirmed that the military had drilled them to be soldiers. For example, even though I had bought each of us some *sadza/pap* (Zimbabwe staple food), I noted that, in collecting their food from the counter, the soldiers respected each other's former military rank. The seniors went first with those of junior rank following. This pattern continued while sitting around the tables. When I asked one of the former soldiers who was a lieutenant in the army, a former platoon commander in the DRC war, why he was sitting at the head of the table, he pointed out: "I am the commander; you know commanders lead and soldiers follow." His response revealed the extent to which the military had conditioned him to think that a distinction exists between those who are commanded and those who command—even in postcombat life.

Because of the intimacies of the stories we shared with each other as former soldiers, I became increasingly interested in conducting research among these men. I revealed to them that I was interested in their stories, particularly their life stories in the military and afterwards. One former soldier asked poignantly, "Why are you interested in issues that you know? We . . . trained together, went to war together, and now we are here together." The question was not an abstract one; indeed it was a methodological question asked by a participant-to-be. I explained that I was interested not only in what happened to us in the military but also in the different meanings each one of us attached to those past military activities. In the end, each soldier agreed to participate, provided I would use pseudonyms. Thus, throughout this article, I use military code names (such as Alpha Romeo, Oscar Papa, Charlie Mike, Sierra Tango, etc.) in presenting my informants' stories of and about the military. Our past military relationship manifested itself when the soldiers promised to take me to their places of residence for the interviews, which they all did. Although I also visited some at their informal work places (in the streets where they worked as street vendors), our relationships continued to develop, and, with their consent, I recorded all of their stories (forty-four in all). While the men's stories revealed many issues about their lives in and after the military, in this article I focus on what military training did to them: shaping them to fit into the military organization, particularly through discipline and punishment.

Welcome to the Military: Stripping the "Civilian Mentality"

While the socialization of military recruits is not uniform across different armies in the world, there are certain practices that most soldiers go through, such as military drills and hazing. In most American and European countries (and in their former colonies), training of recruit soldiers is largely enforced by military orders and commands that mold them into a disciplined and professional force. Thus upon entering the military, the recruit first will read the rules and regulations that will guide him as a soldier. In the first reading one learns what it means to be a soldier serving and defending the sovereignty of the nation (see Woodward 2008). The oath, which can be understood as a representation of the responsibility of soldiers to the nation, is also read. Then, recruits are made to swear allegiance and to affirm to do their military duty diligently upon the order and command of their superiors by appending a signature to the oath as consent to what is contained therein. However, for recruits to truly understand what it means to be a soldier, discipline and punishment are inculcated in the body psyche.

To this end, the military as an organization is akin to what Foucault (1977: 25) refers to as "a system of subjection." Joining the military organization is a "leaving-off" and "taking-on" (Goffman 1961: 20). Clearly, a military organization is not like any other organization where men enter and work. In the military, men are not only trained to work but to conform to and live in a highly structured life. According to Thornborrow and Brown (2011: 355) soldiers are "disciplined by organisationally based discursive resources on which they dr[a]w." For Goffman, the military is a typical example of a total institution. In his definition, "it is a place of residence and work where a large number of like-situated individuals, cut-off from the wider society for an appreciable period of time, together lead an enclosed, formally administered round of life." The specific characteristics that define the military are evident in Goffman's understanding of total institutions: "all aspects of life are conducted in the same place and under the same single authority" (1961: 6). This occurs in the parade square where all drills are expressly conducted in a squared space. Again, "each phase of the members' daily activity is carried on in the immediate company of others, all of whom are treated alike and required to do the same thing together" (Goffman 1961: 6). In short, recruits are trained in platoons and companies each consisting of thirty-five and 105 men, respectively. Activities are coordinated within the group, and no individual effort is celebrated. "All phases of daily activity are tightly scheduled, the whole sequence of activities being imposed from above by a system of explicit formal rulings and a body of officials" (Goffman 1961: 6).

Militarily, this coordination and discipline is represented by a hierarchy of rank and file. An order from the commanding officer goes directly to the lowest rank for execution without questioning. According to Goffman's definition, "the various enforced activities are brought together into a single rational plan purportedly designed to fulfil the officials' aims of the institution" (1961: 6). In short, the singular objective of military training is to make soldiers. This is what Strachan (2006) refers to as the impartation of military grammar. Central to this "making" of soldiers is the use of punishment on recruits. Soldiers are ingrained in the organization; they are "made" through a process of severely enforced military training. As expressed in an interview with "Oscar Papa:"

> On the first day of military training, we dressed in combat uniform. When I went to the mirror to see if it fit me, the military instructor just came in the barrack. He told me that you are not here for modelling. Go out and get inside the pool and roll and crawl from there. I am giving you one minute to complete the task.

Denying a recruit a look in the mirror is an example of particular beliefs that are anchored in "military culture" (see Barrett 1996; Woodward 1998; Lande 2007; Hale 2008). Military culture is a way of life that is fundamentally distinct from civilian organizations. On entering the military institution, recruits are only aware that soldiers go to war; they are not aware of the deep practices that constitute military training. While for these African recruits, civilian life is all about *Ubuntu* (meaning human kindness/humanity toward others), or collective respect for human dignity and being compassionate to others, the military does not adhere to such a civilian understanding of life. Instead, the military has its own "prescription" for making soldiers. It alters the ways African soldiers view people around them. This can be testified by the fact that the sole purpose of the military and of the skills it imparts is legitimate killing; as Caforio (2007) maintains, the sole client of the military is the state. In this case the military is legitimated by the state to train soldiers to be effective killers. And as Hedges (2012: 9) emphasizes, "[W]ar produces killers and . . . organised killing in war is done by a well disciplined and professional army."

Drawing from Goffman (1961), one can say that recruits come to the military with a civilian culture derived from the "home world." For Oscar Papa above, the idea of "looking in the mirror" reveals the "home world," which stands in stark contrast to the "military world." In the military, the bodies of recruits are deprived of rights. As Foucault observes, "the body is caught up in a system of constraints and privations, obligations and prohibitions" (1977: 11). This is evident from the first day of military training, which is quite different from an inauguration or an academic orientation encountered at a university. As interviewee Alpha Sierra notes:

> We were called for a parade and, um, the Commandant officially opened the training and said, "the training is now open, you are now recruits!" After that instructors I heard "prrrrr", they blew the whistle, I am telling you, it was tough because they were making us roll, crawl, you know and we were squeezed and punched on the ground and I am telling you because I still remember, ah, they create certain pools of water and they would say, go there, swim in there and when you come out, you will be wet and instructors say roll on the ground. All recruits' combat uniforms were now full of mud. (Alpha Sierra)

Rolling and crawling reveal how the body is subdued by the military. As Hinojosa (2010) argues, the military is an organization where bodies are transformed. For Foucault, "the systems of punishment are to be situated in a certain political economy of the body" (1977: 25). Thus, the "correction," "control," and transformation of a soldier from a civilian focus on the utility and docility of the body. It is the military body (Woodward and Jenkings 2013) that is an organizational body (Hockey 2002). Because the body is perceived as one that "belongs" to and is "owned" by the military, whistles, which serve as a metaphor of power, are blown to make the body work. Specifically, the whistle represents authority; it gives values but also devalues status positions in a military training field. The whistle values the instructor while devaluing the recruit. This is what Goffman (1961: 15) refers to as "role dispossession," that is, in the context of military training there is "role possession" (that of the instructor), while "role dispossession" is that of the recruit. Thus, the drama of the first day of military training is characterised by the authority of instructors over recruits, including the shoving around of recruits. As such, recruits are subjected to a series of humiliations, abuses, and degradation. According to Alpha Sierra,

> One instructor came to me and said, "you cockroach, go into the muddy pool before I break your naughty assy." So I just put my hands in the pool and sprinkled myself and then I came outside. Then I said, "now I have cheated you." Little did I know that he was watching me. By the time when I crossed the other side of the pool I was just flogged. [laughs] Then he said, "no, go back." (Alpha Sierra)

In the military organization, the recruit "is stripped of the support provided by the home world arrangements" (Goffman 1961: 14). The support of care and love is nonexistent. For Zurcher (1967) civilians are guided by freedom of choice, which cannot be tolerated in the army. In contrast, flogging is often an instrument used during military training, particularly in the first few days when recruits are still gripped by the civilian mentality. Flogging, a habitual practice in many countries' military training, is a symbol of power, representing a relationship between the punisher and the punished. Instructors work on the recruit's body, train it, and force it to carry out tasks. This is what Foucault (1977: 25) refers to as the "political investment of the body"—that is, the body in itself is dominated by instructors and subjected to the wills of the military.

> I am telling you after being flogged, I soaked myself, crawled and mudded along with other recruits. I still remember on my first day, that uniform of mine, on my knees, actually it was, it was torn and tattered on that particular day so that was very tough and, some of the guys, they were wishing that they should have not joined the military. You know the last time I was whipped was when I was at high school. Now instructors were flogging us like hell. Ooh, I still have most of the scratches, the scars of those whips. (Alpha Sierra)

The ways in which instructors work on the body are organised, calculated, and technically thought-out, and thus the subjected body is more than the result of spontaneous practices. Scars on the body are a symbol of the military. They represent a life lived as a recruit as well as the life led by military instructors. Instructors berate recruits: Alpha Romeo remembers the instructor's taunts on the first day of training:

> I still remember the first day of training. I recall when the army instructor said, "for the next coming six months of military training all of you must leave your manhood outside the barracks, and then take it [back] on your pass-out parade, for now it is

only me with a manhood. Did I make myself clear! Squad"! In unison recruits will respond: Sir Yes Sir!

This language of "leaving your manhood outside the barracks" illustrates that recruits are emasculated by military instructors. In terms of Foucauldian analysis, figures in authority use derogatory language to express their specific dominance and at the same time to exact particular obedience from those they dominate. At this point, the "undignified" language used by instructors is intentional. It is a weapon of power in the transformation process. Derogatory language reflects power relations that exist between instructors and recruits. It sharpens and "toughens" the mind (Gibson 2010). It is embedded and ingrained in soldiers' behaviors as their organizational language. According to Arkin and Dobrofysky (1978), "[V]erbal practices are used by drill instructors to train recruits to withstand stress." Thus derogatory language, like every step and command during hazing, has a military purpose.

> We were asked to shave our heads, our beard. One of my instructors nicknamed Ninja told us that a recruit soldier's shaved head must shine like the bum of a newly born baby. After that the instructor asked us to balance upside-down on our clean shaven heads at night while singing the national anthem until morning (Charlie Mike)

While the "civilian body" is that which is perceived as a "feminine body," the military conquers that body and remolds it into a "military body" (see Hockey 2002). This is what Foucault (1977: 26) refers to as "the political technology of the body." Such processes are viewed as part of military initiation, a welcoming into the military organization. For Zurcher (1967) military training disorientates and reorientates recruits. The army seeks to control and transform recruits' bodies through a detailed surveillance of their activities (see McSorley 2013; Newlands 2013).

> Throughout the first seven days of military training we were not allowed to sleep. One instructor nicknamed Doctor, because of [his] expertise in hazing recruits told us that the military is a field of pain- no one is going to rescue you, but you will rescue yourselves by doing what we order you to do. We spent the first seven nights singing, it was called "deep freezing" period meaning that it was a tough period of crawling and rolling in the mud. (Bravo Mike)

Throughout the "deep-freezing" period, recruits' bodies were soaked to the skin, wet and muddied. Because the hazing of recruits is intended to instill them with a new military mentality, where pain is celebrated by the trained man, in the first days of military training recruits are immersed in water, soaked to the skin, made to crawl and to roll until their fatigues are torn to rags. This idea of "deep freezing" is the first stage in military training, separating potential recruits from "visitors," those recruits who are not sure whether or not they want to join the military but are, instead, interested in weighing their objections, in the training camp. Lima Delta talks about how he found ways to sleep during military training:

> When I grew up I didn't know that actually somebody can sleep, seated straight [up] when it is raining, but actually I learnt during training that even when it is raining, when it is pouring, I can sit in the middle of the rain, I will not be feeling that rain. I slept because that was the only time I would get. If I can sleep for 10 to 20 minutes it's enough during training. Sometimes I can just go to the toilet, ask to go to the toilet then I can sit on the chamber and sleep but, when the instructor caught me it would be again another punishment. (Lima Delta)

Being denied sleep trains recruits in the reality that the military is a twenty-four hour, seven days a week, occupation, particularly during war. Punishment is meted out to those who attempt to dodge this. According to Hockey (2002: 150), the body is controlled by a training program that is akin to a perpetual conveyor belt proceeding at a hectic pace. The idea of sleeping for ten to twenty minutes is not a choice for recruits; rather it is an initiative to deal with the situation in the training sessions. The whole intention is to weed out the feeble and weave together the real recruits, and it is usually only after these first hazing phases that the military will start issuing military equipment to the new recruits.

Such military equipment, including guns, is the symbol of a soldier, representing the soldier and the military as an organization. This is what Woodward and Jenkings (2011) call the materiality between the gun and the soldier, in which soldiers' identities are understood and framed through the use of such weapons. Interestingly, however, the first time a gun is issued, this is also characterised by punishment. A soldier has to be both man enough to do what the gun does and be disciplined when holding a gun. Thus military instructors instil both modalities—courage and discipline—and the latter is characterised by punishment:

> When we signed for our rifles, the first thing we were told was to squat on them, raising our hands up while singing the national anthem. When we failed to sing in unison, the instructor ordered us to raise our rifles above our heads, singing (Tango Papa).

The idea of holding a rifle in one hand while the other hand grasps the crotch is itself a punishment. For Foucault (1977: 93) "punishment is an art of effects . . . and it looks towards the future . . . that one must punish exactly enough to prevent repetition." Since the relationship between soldiers and guns is one that is forged through punishment, this affects a soldier's understanding of his rifle. In a metaphorical sense, the weapon is an extension of the soldier's body (see Mankayi 2008; Woodward and Jenkings 2013). Recruits are punished so they can conform to a military way of doing and being. The holding of rifles for the first time goes along with a symbolic representation, that of singing the national anthem, which means that the men are ready to train to defend the nation.

> I have never felt so exhausted like what happened to me when we were commanded to carry 20kg sandbags on our backs, coupled with an AK rifle. We could then be ordered to run along the railway line. (Sierra Mike)

The training of soldiers for war purposes is what Woodward (2000) refers to as the making of "warrior heroes." It is a period in which pain is synonymous with gain (Higate 2000). The physicality of military training has to do with making a soldierly body—that is, a body that can fight in war terrains. For Higate (2000), training is meant to produce men of valor and strength.

> From the field craft where we were taught the theory of being a soldier, you go to assault course where you do the practical of crossing obstacles like climbing over high walls, crawling in a 400m mudded tunnel, crawling under barbed wire. (Yankee Golf)

In short, becoming a soldier is embedded in both theory and practice. Learning how to become a soldier through field craft lessons is not enough; one has to immerse oneself in the practical terrain that is synonymous with the real battlefield. Thus, while the process of shaping the recruits begins with hazing during field craft activities, importantly, the military places great emphasis on the drill that follows.

Word of Command: Drills, Dressing, and Discipline

At the center of the parade square is the drill instructor who represents what Foucault (1977: 125) refers to as a "machine for altering minds." One of the most formidable activities which are said to "alter" and make a soldier is drill, which is conducted by word of command. The recruits are taught how to crawl and roll in the mud, climb over walls, and cross flooded rivers, but drill is quite a different activity. Drill transforms a harnessed body into a disciplined body. It teaches a soldier how to listen and take orders as he is given by the word of command. When a soldier is ordered to march quickly or slowly and to halt, there are no questions; the orders must be obeyed. Drill teaches soldiers how to march in unison, in groups. According to Arkin and Dobrofysky (1978: 160) "inspections and drills form the strong, silent, obedient man." The first thing that a soldier is taught is how to dress for such drills. As one interviewee recalled:

> I was taught how to dress in a military way, my combat shirt must be in my underwear, the denim (combat trouser) must be tightened with my patrol boots, I must be cleanly shaven, I must only leave 3 buttons of my shirts outside. Above all my patrol boots must be shining, the shoes must be like a mirror, reflecting my image. (Alpha Romeo)

Teaching men how to dress for drill represents particular discipline and uniformity in the military. Drill is a symbol of discipline, which is an organizational value. It conditions recruits to respond obediently to commands (see Hockey 2002). There is constant surveillance of how recruit soldiers dress and wear combat uniforms to embed them as members of the military organization. For Foucault (1977: 129), "the agent of punishment must exercise a total power. . . .[T]he individual to be corrected must be entirely enveloped in the power that is being exercised over him."

The most difficult thing to be taught is how to march. Oscar Papa revealed how the word of command is not always clear on what to do; it is a military language that one is not familiar with, given by an instructor who always uses a loud voice. For example,

> Recruits today is your first day in the parade square where I am going to teach you how to march in both quick and slow march. Any one of you who is not going to get me clear must let me know, Squad! . . . As I lift my right leg about 45cm from the ground, thigh parallel to the ground, I return it in this way (instructor demonstrating). If I say quick march, it is always your left foot that must go first, the same is on slow march. (Victor Tango)

The parade square is a "sacred" place where coughing, sneezing, and fidgeting are totally prohibited and punished. For Foucault (1977: 135), soldiers are taught to "stand upright . . . holding their heads high and erect . . . never to fix their eyes on the ground, but to look straight at those they pass." On parade, recruits/soldiers learn how to take and execute an order. This is yet another example of the "programming" of recruits into soldiers within the military system. The ways in which the soldiers respond is defined by bodily practice, which is ingrained by repetition. Being taught how to quick and slow march is quite intentional in the sense that it is fundamental in the making of disciplined soldiers. This, according to Foucault (1977: 137), produces "docile" bodies—ones that are malleable enough to be reshaped, subjected, improved, and transformed. Importantly from a Foucauldian analysis, discipline is a general formula of domination that transforms the confused into ordered multiplicities (see 1977: 146). Thus, drill shapes a subjected collective group within the military. Drills are characterised by inspection of the body and of dressing. In such activities "social distance is typically great and formally prescribed, talk is conducted in high voice" (Goffman 1961: 7). Whisky Papa reveals how and what the instructors inspect. Those found to be dirty are punished.

> The parade square is where we were inspected in a drill formation, i.e. one arm distance from each other. I remember this instructor once said to me, "you have a dirty nose! Dirty big Assy! Dirty shoe!" And finally he said, "you are a Dirty human being!" You know when I think of it I laugh but during that time it was a moment of madness, it was a serious business! I was always punished. You know the instructor will just say go and water yourself and crawl from the water point.

Inspection as a military practice controls, corrects, and disciplines the operation of the body. It is a "technique of surveillance" that represents "physics of power" (see Foucault 1977: 172). During inspections, the whole body has to conform to the prescribed roles. Instructors understand that the submission of the recruit body to the military is a productive process, which at the end of military training produces a useful and intelligible body, particularly in a war context. Thus, through disciplining and punishing the body, a new body is born, not only for the growth of skills or to intensify its subjection, but as the body becomes more obedient, it becomes more useful (Foucault 1977: 138). On reflection, "moments of madness" can later be perceived as moments of laughter. The price of inspection of the recruit's body in the military is accompanied by punishment to conform. For Goffman, soldiers are not supervised, rather "surveillance is employed to oversee if everyone does what is expected of him" (1961: 7). Inspecting with intent to punish is what Foucault refers to as "techniques of punishment" (1977: 126). Thus, inspection in the military is synonymous with discipline and, most importantly, with punishment. An inspection of the body means that the body itself has to be regulated and regimented according to military standards. Through inspection the body is manipulated and shaped. It becomes a skillful and tactical body. For Newlands (2013), soldiers are constantly inspected so that their bodies can become habituated to the military. The whole idea is "to shape the total person into being a disciplined cog in the military machine" (see Arkin and Dobrofysky 1978: 158).

In addition to inspection, flogging is also used to "shape the total person." For Oscar Papa

> Being beaten in the military is the order of the day. It's like when you are not beaten, you wonder what is going to happen, why am I not yet beaten. Actually it came to a point that we have to be beaten or there is certain punishment that instructors have to give us. So if we spend a day without any being flogged, we would be worried about what's next so it was very tough. (Oscar Papa)

According to Foucault (1977: 136), the body is an object and target of power. Recruits are made to understand the habitual practice of flogging as part of their being. There is a "knifing-off of past civilian life" (Zurcher 1967). In doing so, the military "reforges a new biography." This reveals how punishment itself becomes part of the recruit life in which it becomes ingrained. In economic terms, discipline increases the productive nature of the body, but in political terms it increases obedience (Foucault 1977). Flogging is meant to enforce conformity. According to Arkin and Dobrofysky (1978), conformity to the prescribed rules of conduct is the focal point for change within the military processes of indoctrination. Thus, what is meant to conform is the body, which is not at rest during the process of military training.

> Sometimes during the night instructors would just give you a certain task which is senseless because, for example, there was an abandoned airstrip close to our training area. Instructors ordered us to dig that abandoned airstrip, you know. For what reason you are not supposed to know, because they just wanted to keep you busy, you know, just to remove a civilian mentality. They were training us not to question the command . . . but by the end of the day we ended up enjoying [it] (Lima India).

The idea of learning how to obey orders is done in often unexpected ways—ways that are painful to the body. Thus it is not only the body that must obey the command, but the mind must conform as well. There are no mathematical calculations at recruit training. Charlie Mike emphasized that "1+1 is not 2 in the military." There is no exact time for a certain activity. Military activities are punctuated neither by time nor weather, but by order and command.

> We were taught in a tough way, we were taught a certain level of discipline, we were taught a certain level of understanding and we were taught a certain level of endurance. I can say endurance was the main thing that we were being taught because we find that actually some of the situations that they were making us to go through, they were not actually hurting us, but they wanted to prepare us for future purposes. At times we could queue for food while jogging (double march) and singing and then ordered to eat in two minutes, while the food was hot. I can face like a certain tough

situation in my life that actually a normal, a common human being cannot go through it. (Charlie Mike)

Similarly, Foucault (1977: 26) argues that "the power exercised on the body is conceived not as a property, but as a strategy, that its effects of domination are attributed not to appropriation, but to dispositions, manoeuvres, tactics, techniques and functioning." Many years after military training, soldiers reflect, often in a positive manner, on the ways they were trained. Thus the subjected body is now seen as a productive body. These are the positives of a once-subjected body to the military: one that can now endure beyond what a civilian can. According to Foucault (1977: 202–203), when individuals regulate their own behaviors, they are self-disciplining. Such awareness is linked to the physical training of a soldier that prepares him for exercises outside the barracks. Each of the phases has its tactical approaches:

> Outside the barracks, in our final training exercise, we were taught how to advance attack and withdraw in war. In our defence exercise, we advanced for 86km in a game park full of elephants and lions. We advanced for three consecutive days and nights. We deployed for two weeks, and then withdrew. It was an exercise we did in a desert-like area, there was no water, the situation taught us to be soldiers. (Oscar Tango)

Training exercises both in and outside the barracks speak to how the military makes soldiers fit into both worlds: the barracks and the bush, where it is desert-like. Woodward (1998) reveals how the little green outside the barracks fits in the soldierly world. However, even though there are constant deprivations in the military, recruits spoke about certain parts of military training that were much easier to go through than others. An example of this was when a former platoon commander, Charlie Delta, who once served as a senior officer military instructor, talked about map reading as a part of jungle exercises that was easily accepted by recruits. He notes that "generally recruits enjoy the freedom that comes with map reading, they find it less painful because they are just deployed in a jungle; they do map reading, and they can decide when to cook and eat from their ration packs" (Charlie Delta).

This example of map reading presents binaries of "freedom" and "oppression." While the former is a complete characteristic of being at "home," the latter presents what military barracks can do to recruit soldiers, working under the eye of the military instructor. However, soldiers do not simply wait for those "freedom" moments to come; rather they also come to evade military order and instructions differently.

Evading Command and Control

Despite the conformity of recruit soldiers to military training instruction, there are also moments of resistance to orders and command. However, it is important to note that such resistance to military instruction is subtle, as Golf Charlie reveals: "Because instructors would force us to carry 20 kg of sand at the back of our pouches, sometimes we would just put two loaves of bread, zip it [up] and it appears as if it's sand." While such resistance to military instruction and order is a punishable offence if discovered by an officer, this phenomenon is also highly celebrated, especially by recruits who perceive it as a tactic of resistance. This tactic of carrying two loaves of bread rather than the required twenty kilograms of sand is an initiative celebrated by recruit soldiers. Similarly, in his writing about British infantry soldiers, Hockey (2002: 152) reveals that at certain moments recruits employ corporeal tactics to counter bodily control during military training. The purpose of such tactics is the counter manipulation of their bodies in both real and symbolic terms. In revealing his experience as a platoon commander, Bravo Charlie speaks to this: "Inasmuch as you want to train recruits to endure hunger as a way to prepare . . . for war, at night some recruits always sneak out, dress in civilian clothing, and buy food at the nearby shops." Thus, while recruits "accept" military instructions as part of transforming them into soldiers, points of resistance also exist. Interestingly, such practices of circumventing military orders by recruits can also be seen as part of soldiering, for example, the ability to move from point A to point B on the battlefield without being seen by the enemy. It follows that, while we understand the making of soldiers as a practice that emanates from the top—from training that comes from military instructors, soldiers are also produced from below, by evading military orders. In the barracks, soldiers refer to this practice of evading command as "skiving," literally meaning dodging command. Hockey defines skiving as "making the body as invisible as possible to superiors." Accordingly, within the barracks, routes that maximize concealment to avoid the centers of power, such as battalion headquarters, which house individuals who embody disciplinary power, are used (Hockey 2002: 153). Interestingly both military training as well as its evasion through skiving teaches soldiers to execute their combative duties.

We Lived like Bums

There is nothing more important in the army than the feeling of being part of a large combat group. Strong feelings of being part of a military unit are forged through struggle. Because one of the core focuses of the military is to enforce teamwork, it follows that an attempt is made to erase ethnic differences as much as possible. In the Zimbabwean context, where the majority of recruit soldiers were divided along two main ethnic groups, the Ndebele and Shona, the military dealt with these differences by partnering a Ndebele and Shona recruit in carrying out military tasks. As Victor Tango reveals, "[W]hen I entered the military, I had no Shona friend[s], but the military made me to have not only one but many Shona friends." Lima Bravo added, "[F]rom the first day of military training we were instructed that in the military there are no Ndebele or Shona people, but there are soldiers ready to fight." This "military spirit" is indoctrinated through hazing by military instructors during training. According to Harrison and Laliberte (1994), the military inculcates a "willing spirit." The bond is made possible because military life emphasizes living separately from civilians, wearing a distinct uniform, and having a barracks hospital, shops, and club—all of which facilitate closeness among soldiers. For Winslow (1994), individual effort is suppressed and invested into the group. How military bonding emanates and what it does is summed up by one Canadian soldier's words:

> You have a bond. You have a bond that's so thick that it is unbelievable!...It's the pull, it's the team, the work as a team, the team spirit! I don't think that ever leaves a guy. That is exactly what basic training is supposed to do. It is supposed to weed out those who aren't willing to work that way . . . And that's the whole motivation that when somebody says we want you to do something then you'll do it. You will do it because of the team, for the team, with the team and because the team has the same focus (Harrison and Laliberte (1994: 28).

Bonding is perceived as the spirit embedded within an individual soldier for the collective. For Hynes (2001) military bonds are much more important than friendship as the former are framed within combative duties. A soldier lives for the team and the team becomes the focal point in combat. As Hedges (2012: 7) argues, "[W]ar gives a sense that soldiers can raise above their divisiveness. . . .[T]he march against the enemy generates an unfamiliar bond, with the desire to kill." This kind of bonding intensifies in postcombat life partly because of nostalgia, including wistful bonding in the aftermath of "active" military life and reminiscing of days past.

In short, the military presents a cohesive organization in which the collective is much more important than the individual. It is a team, and individuals work for the success of the unit. In order to achieve that cohesiveness, the military puts great emphasis on such bonds, which Oscar Papa accentuates by using a bodily metaphor:

> We were taught that we soldiers—we live like bums. You know when bums sit, they sit together, when you walk, bums are intact and they are equal. Bums look alike, none is bigger or smaller. (Oscar Papa)

The use of this metaphor—bums, as in one's backside—by Oscar Papa represents how these bonds are humanized and valued. The metaphor reveals how such bonds are accorded a life, lived, and maintained in the present. Military bonds are a result of deep bodily and knowledge connections, "one body"—which is vital for survival in times of war. The use of "bums" by instructors to depict sameness/comradeship or brotherhood reveals what Foucault (1977: 28) calls the "body politic." In addition, the use of bums reveals that recruits' bodies are subjugated by turning them into objects of knowledge. Thus bonding is also a metaphor of power in the military—that is, bonds do not just spontaneously develop but are the result of rigorous coercive power relations in the exercise of duty. For Foucault (1977: 26) "power is not exercised simply as an obligation or a prohibition on those 'who do not have it.'" Thus those who are perceived not to have power actually have power in some ways to act on and for them—in this case through bonding. Such connections in the military represent what Wenger (1998) calls a "community of practice," members bound together by common interests, values, and beliefs. According to Charlie Mike,

> In the military, regardless of the language you speak, you have to be united. You know during our first days we were still having that mentality, that mentality of home, the civilian mentality that actually no, this one is not my brother, I am not related to him so even if we can be given a task, it will be very difficult to complete that task together because I have my own view and that particular person has his own view. By the end of the day we argue but I am telling you, we were trained to be united, they taught us unity and that served a long, a long way because you understand that actually in the military, when you are in the warzone, sometimes when a fellow soldier is shot you cannot leave him, you have to carry him but if you are not trained to do that, if they don't instil that unity in you, you cannot perform those things. (Charlie Mike)

Having such a bond with other soldiers is about love, loyalty, and dedication. As Dowling (2011) emphasizes, it is an unbreakable bond. It is difficult for this kind of bond to be recreated, because it is not just about the experience of war but the many intense hours of training and preparation that comprise a soldier's life. Bonding captures the emotion of the experience, draws you into the scene, and makes you feel like another soldier is your blood brother, and leaving other soldiers behind, for example, on the battlefield is impossible.

> On pass-out day, I felt confident in my mind, but most importantly, my body had changed, it was now a soldier's body. When I went back home on two weeks off days, the way my sisters talked was purely civilian, the way they eat was of civilians, even the way they laughed was civilian. I find it difficult to talk to them in greater detail, I wanted to be around my comrades in arms, I was always thinking about the barrack. I felt I was now part of the military. My former friends were no longer interesting to me. (Yankee India)

Such views reveal that the military is a very possessive organization. It does not want to share its principles, values, and beliefs with the outside world—the civilian world. As Segal (1986: 10) points out, the military is a typical "greedy institution" that depends for its survival on the loyalty, participation, and commitment of its members. In short, the military is one of a few institutions where men who enter as civilians with a "civilian mentality" exist with a changed mind—one that has erased their former beliefs.

Conclusion

In this article I have described how the military forges a relationship with and between soldiers through techniques of discipline and punishment, using the Zimbabwe military as a case study. The "civilian mentality" is stripped away from the recruit and is replaced by the "military mentality." I have emphasized that the stripping of this "civilian mentality" is no easy job. It requires rigorous discipline and punishment to conform, and ultimately transform, the recruit into a soldier. Thus discipline and punishment inculcate military organizational life in soldiers and they become embedded in the organization. The military focuses on both the mind and body to make soldiers out of civilians. Military training is practice, imbued with the subjection of the body to the organization. Recruits are made to understand what it means for them to be in a military organization. Such processes are "tough," but the end product is a soldier who carries with him a "military body" meant to resist the tests of war. Soldiers leave behind their civilian understanding of society, one that respects human dignity/kindness, and they embrace a military culture that subscribes to the legitimate use of violence and specializes in killing. A hierarchy of order and command is imposed on recruits and, through the process of disciplining and punishment, soldiers are made into a cohesive unit. However, as I have argued, the process of "making" soldiers is not one of total oppression: recruits can evade punishment through "skiving," employing their own counter tactics, getting socialized from below, and thereby becoming even better soldiers.

Note

1. Acknowledgement is made to the anonymous reviewers for their insightful comments and suggestions. The author is a VolkswagenStiftung postdoctoral fellow at the University of the Western Cape. The writing of this article was made possible by support from the Social Science Research Council's Next Generation Social Sciences in Africa, with funds provided by the Carnegie Corporation of New York, a PhD research award from the University of Peace—International Development Research Centre (UPEACE—IDRC), and the VolkswagenStiftung Post-Doctoral Fellowship Award.

References

Alao, Abiodun. 1995. "The Metamorphosis of the 'Unorthodox': The Integration and Early Development of the Zimbabwe National Army." Pp. 104–117 in Ngwabi Bhebe and T.O. Ranger, eds. *Soldiers in Zimbabwe's Liberation War*. London: James Currey.

Alexander, Jocelyn. 1998. "Dissident Perspectives on Zimbabwe's Post-independence War." *Journal of the International Africa Institute* 68(2):151–182.

Alexander, Jocelyn. 2013. "Militarisation and State Institutions: 'Professionals' and 'Soldiers' inside the Zimbabwe Prison Service." *Journal of Southern African Studies* 39(4):807–828.

Arkin, William and Lynne R. Dobrofsky. 1978. "Military Socialization and Masculinity." *Journal of Social Issues* 34(1):151–168.

Barrett, Frank J. 1996. "The Organizational Construction of Hegemonic Masculinity: The Case of the US Navy." *Gender, Work & Organization* 3(3):129–142.

Caforio, Giuseppe. 2007. "Introduction: The Interdisciplinary and Cross-national Character of Social Studies on the Military—The Need for Such an Approach." Pp. 1–20 in Giuseppe Caforio, ed. *Social Sciences and the Military: An Interdisciplinary Overview*. London & New York: Routledge.

Dowling, Mike. 2011. *Sergeant Rex: The Unbreakable Bond between a Marine and his Military Working Dog*. New York: Atria Books.

Foucault, Michel. 1977. *Discipline and Punish: The Birth of the Prison*. New York: Vintage Books.

Gibson, Diana. 2010. "Construction of Masculinity, Mental Toughness and the Inexpressibility of Distress among a Selected Group of South African Veterans of the 'Bush War' in Namibia." *Journal of Psychology in Africa* 20(4):613–622.

Goffman, Ervin. 1961. *Asylums: Essays on the Social Situation of Mental Patients and Other Inmates*. Chicago: Aldine

Hale, Hannah C. 2008. "The Development of British Military Masculinities through Symbolic Resources." *Culture & Psychology* 14(3):305–332.

Harrison, Deborah and Lucie Laliberte. 1994. *No Life Like It: Military Wives in Canada*. Toronto: James Lorimer.

Hedge, Chris. 2012. *War is a Force that Gives Us Meaning*. New York: Public Affairs.

Higate, Paul R. 2000. "Tough Bodies and Rough Sleeping: Embodying Homelessness Amongst Ex-servicemen." *Housing, Theory and Society* 17(3):97–108.

Higate, Paul R. and Alisa Cameron. 2006. "Reflexivity and Researching the Military." *Armed Forces & Society* 32(2):219–233.

Hinojosa, Ramon. 2010. "Doing Hegemony: Military, Men, and Constructing a Hegemonic Masculinity." *Journal of Men's Studies* 18(2):179–194.

Hockey, John. 2002. "Head Down, Bergen on, Mind in Neutral: The Infantry Body." *Journal of Political and Military Sociology* 30(1):148–171.

Hynes, Samuel L. 2001. *The Soldiers' Tale: Bearing Witness to Modern War.* New York: Allen Lane, The Penguin Press.

Jackson, Paul. 2011. "The Civil War Roots of Military Domination in Zimbabwe: The Integration Process following the Rhodesian War and the Road to ZANLA Dominance." *Civil Wars* 13(4):371–395.

Lande, Brian. 2007. "Breathing Like a Soldier: Culture Incarnate." *Sociological Review* 55(1):95–108.

Mankayi, Nyameka. 2008. "Masculinity, Sexuality and the Body of Male Soldiers." *Psychology in Society* 36:24–44.

McSorley, Kevin. 2013. "Introduction". Pp. 1–32 in Kevin McSorely, ed. *War and the Body: Militarisation, Practice and Experience.* London: Routledge.

Newlands, Emma. 2013. "Preparing and Resisting the War Body: Training in the British Army." Pp. 35–50 in Kevin McSorely, ed. *War and the Body: Militarisation, Practice and Experience.* London: Routledge.

Ranger, Terrence. 2004. "Nationalist Historiography, Patriotic History and the History of the Nation: The Struggle over the Past in Zimbabwe." *Journal of Southern African Studies* (30)2:215–234.

Segal, Mady W. 1986. "The Military and the Family as Greedy Institutions." *Armed Forces & Society* 13(1):9–38.

Strachan, Hew. 2006. "Training, Morale and Modern War." *Journal of Contemporary History* 41(2):211–227.

Tendi, Blessing-Miles. 2008. "Patriotic History and Public Intellectuals Critical of Power." *Journal of Southern African Studies* 34(2):379–396.

Tendi, Blessing-Miles. 2013. "Ideology, Civilian Authority and the Zimbabwean Military." *Journal of Southern African Studies* 39(4):829–843.

Thornborrow, Thomas and Andrew D. Brown. 2009. "Being Regimented: Aspiration, Discipline and Identity Work in the British Parachute Regiment." *Organisation Studies* 30(3):355–376.

Wenger, Etienne. 1998. *Communities of Practice: Learning, Meaning and Identity.* Cambridge: Cambridge University Press.

White, Luise. 2007. "Whoever Saw a Country with Four Armies?: The Battle of Bulawayo Revisited." *Journal of Southern African Studies* 33(3):619–631.

Winslow, Donna. 1994. "Rites of Passage and Group Bonding in the Canadian Airborne." *Armed Forces & Society* 25(3):429–457.

Woodward, Rachel. 1998. "'It's a Man's Life!': Soldiers, Masculinity and the Countryside." *Gender, Place & Culture* 5(3)277–300.

Woodward, Rachel. 2000. "Warrior Heroes and Little Green Men: Soldiers, Military Training, and the Construction of Rural Masculinities." *Rural Sociology* 65(4):640–657.

Woodward, Rachel. 2008. "'Not for the Queen and Country or any of that Shit. . .': Reflection on Citizenship and Military Participation in Contemporary British Soldier Narratives." Pp. 363–384 in Emily Gilbert and Deborah Cowan, eds. *War, Citizenship, Territory.* London: Routledge.

Woodward, Rachel and K. Neil Jenkings. 2011. "Military Identities in the Situated Accounts of British Military Personnel." *Sociology* 45(2):252–268.

Woodward, Rachel and K. Neil Jenkings. 2013. "Soldiers' Bodies and the Contemporary British Military Memoir." Pp. 152–164 in Kevin McSorely, ed. *War and the Body: Militarisation, Practice and Experience.* London: Routledge.

Young, Ernest T. 1997. "Chefs and worried Soldiers: Authority and Power in the Zimbabwe National Army." *Armed Forces & Society* 24(1):133–149.

Zurcher, Louis A. 1967. "The Naval Recruit Centre: A Study of Role Assimilation in a Total Institution." *Sociological Inquiry* 37(1):85–98.

Book Reviews

Talking about Torture: How Political Discourse Shapes the Debate by Jared Del Rosso. New York: Columbia University Press, 2015 (276 pages; cloth).

Reviewed by Stephanie Athey
Lasell College

University of Denver sociologist Jared Del Rosso undertakes a methodical analysis of public documents that few citizens are likely to read. The result is a significant and accessible narrative account of the shifts and contours in a debate among US political elites and elected officials as they sparred over the meaning and reality of torture.

Del Rosso draws on published transcripts of forty-two congressional hearings on detention and interrogation policy held between 2003 and 2008. With detailed attention to language and context, and an effective argument about the significance of political language to a study of violence itself, he demonstrates that this abundance of political "talk about torture" constructed and reconstructed the meaning of violence and its symbolic weight for the nation.

The book is to be commended for devoting attention to abuses beyond those photographed at the prison in Abu Ghraib, Iraq. House and Senate responses to Abu Ghraib are analyzed here but so are committee debates over a range of other claims. Of particular interest are the discussion of abusive detentions of citizens and foreigners in Brooklyn's Metropolitan Detention Center shortly after September 11, 2001; Donald Rumsfeld's interrogation protocols for Mohammed al-Qahtani at Guantanamo Bay; and the rhetorical high-wire act performed by Lt. Gen. Randall M. Schmidt as he defended aggressive and bizarre "gender coercion" at Guantanamo, holding it—remarkably—to be consistent with long-held military interrogation standards. Here too

is a fine-grained examination of conflicting congressional interpreta-
tions of the waterboard in CIA hands after the disclosure that the CIA
had destroyed video evidence.

In the latter, Del Rosso points up how the congressional dispute dif-
fered sharply *only* over the effectiveness of the waterboard and whether
its use could really be controlled, clinical, and restrained (not brutish and
excessive and, therefore, torture). These distinctions inevitably *affirmed*
the premise that limited, controlled, and effective uses of state violence
can be acceptable. In this, the torture debate paved a smooth road for
the transition from Bush to Obama, where torture of suspects in detention gave way to drone strikes on suspects in the open air. Purportedly
limited, controlled and effective, such strikes eliminate the need for
detention at all.

The book argues that whether contentious congressional hearings
ultimately construed particular claims, episodes, or sites of torture/abuse
to be national crises or instead held them to be minor actions consistent
with military standards was a function of at least three powerful elements:
(a) the organizational power invested in the committee chair, (b) the varied
forms and quality of emerging documentary evidence that accumulated
across this period, and (c) an ever-changing political context. That political context was marked by the waning rhetorical utility of recourse to
the "urgency of September 11, 2001," presidential and midterm election
cycles, new decisions by the Supreme Court, and wavering public support for wars in Afghanistan and Iraq.

Del Rosso's analysis of contending congressional claims about vio-
lence is informed by research on the sociological construction of social
problems, on state denial of atrocity, and on the practice of torture.
The study builds in particular on important volumes by Darius Rejali
(*Torture and Democracy*, Princeton, 2007), Stanley Cohen (*States of
Denial*, Blackwell, 2001), and a study by Physicians for Human Rights
entitled *Broken Laws, Broken Lives: Medical Evidence of Torture by U.S.
Personnel and Its Impact – A Report* (2008). This important, latter study
profiles eleven survivors of US torture practice, brings their testimony
into the public record, and offers medical documentation of their claims.

In an appendix, Del Rosso takes up matters of disciplinary interest
to social scientists and survivors. He notes that, in the social sciences
more broadly, the disciplinary call to "bracket" reality in order to focus
on *processes* of claims making can generate false neutrality toward
torture claims. In the context of suffering, an "objective" or bracketed
approach can serve to multiply uncertainty, an outcome that inevitably

weighs against the survivor and supports the work of state denial. Here he speaks to concerns, ones he shares, that the approach of researchers who work through a constructionist lens can be disturbing, even an affront, to antitorture workers who struggle for public and political recognition of the "reality" of torture and the moral, medical, and legal claims of torture survivors.

In the face of such nuanced and urgent problems of approach, this volume is determinedly alert to moments when meaning "idled" between different interpretive frameworks and a dominant narrative on torture might have taken an alternative route. *Talking about Torture* is written to highlight those conditions under which antitorture politics might advance and thrive, and denial is most effectively opposed. The volume will be of great interest to a broad spectrum of citizens and scholars.

***

Waging War, Planning Peace: U.S. Noncombat Operations and Major Wars by Aaron Rapport. Ithaca: Cornell University Press, 2015 (266 pages; paper).

Reviewed by Liam Collins
United States Military Academy

In his book, *Waging War, Planning Peace*, Aaron Rapport analyzes the strategic assessments of the costs and risks associated with noncombat operations that coincide with major combat operations. The noncombat operations he is particularly interested in explaining are state building activities, those often associated with "post combat" operations or more commonly known as "Phase IV" operations following the Iraq War. He finds existing explanations—including cultural, organizational, and civil-military theories—lacking, so he turns to the field of psychology for a better explanation. In a similar manner that Jack Levy brought prospect theory to international relations scholars more than twenty years ago, Rapport now introduces construal level theory (CLT) to international relations scholars and makes a compelling case for the utility of using CLT to understand the strategic assessments of policymakers.

CLT is a social psychology theory that describes the relationship between psychological distance and people's thinking: distant events are thought of abstractly, closer events are thought of concretely. With an abstract construal, individuals consider the bigger picture (the ends); with a concrete construal, individuals focus on the details of the task (the means). By applying CLT to combat and noncombat operations, Rapport can explain why US officials have repeatedly struggled with state building operations. According to CLT, strategic assessments should be influenced by temporal distance. Assessments for events thought to occur in the near term focus on feasibility, while those thought to occur in the more distant future focus on the desirability of the goals or policy objectives. Since noncombat operations are thought of as temporally distant to combat operations they are assessed abstractly; this leads to overconfidence and a lack of detail as to how the operations will actually be executed. However, Rapport also postulates that officials only assess noncombat operations abstractly if they have long term goals. In other words, the more transformative the objectives, the more likely officials are to think abstractly; if they are only trying to maintain the status quo, they are more likely to think concretely.

Rapport turns to the cases of the US occupation of Germany, "Phase IV" and the invasion of Iraq, state building during the escalation in Vietnam, and the "occupation that never was" in Korea, to test CLT. He makes a fairly compelling argument that CLT does a better job at explaining the actions of policymakers than other explanations such as opportunity cost, the "fog of war" and the nature of the operation, organizational, and civil-military explanations. CLT is able to explain why officials in the Roosevelt administration during WWII and the Bush administration during the Iraq War were initially overly optimistic about noncombat operations and then shifted to a concrete construal as major combat operations came to an end. Both wars had transformational goals for the region and thus, most officials' assessments were abstract and they underestimated the cost and difficulty of state building operations. By contrast US leaders' construal was primarily concrete for Korea and Vietnam since most viewed the conflicts as a way to maintain the status quo. Thus, they were more focused on the feasibility of noncombat operations rather than the desirability of policy goals. Nonetheless, Rapport uses CLT to demonstrate that a concrete construal brings its own set of problems: officials may be so focused on the task at hand that it becomes an end to itself, often disconnected from the larger goal.

Overall, Rapport presents a fairly compelling argument. He readily admits CLT has some shortcomings, in that personality traits sometimes better explain the assessments of some officials than does a temporal construal, but on the whole, CLT does a better job explaining the assessment of government actors than other explanations. If the book has its shortcomings, it is a lack of recommendations. His theory would seem to forebode a negative prospect for any noncombat operation. Policymakers either have a long time horizon, resulting in overconfidence, or they have a short time horizon, focusing on means to the exclusion of ends. Given this challenge, more time should have been devoted to recommendations. Nonetheless, this work is an important contribution to understanding why US policymakers have repeatedly struggled with state building and brings CLT to the field of international relations. In sum, this book is well worth reading and if it forces policymakers to think more about the feasibility of the operation rather than the desirability of the goals, then it is possible that some costly endeavors in the future might be avoided.

The views expressed by the reviewer do not necessarily reflect those of the United States Military Academy, the Department of Defense, or the US Government.

The Markets for Force: Privatization of Security Across World Regions edited by Molly Dunigan and Ulrich Petersohn. Philadelphia: University of Pennsylvania Press, 2015 (224 pages; cloth).

Reviewed by Renée de Nevers
Syracuse University

The popular impression of private security is one of gun-toting bodyguards swaggering through high-threat environments. This book helps illuminate the much broader range of activities undertaken by a diverse set of actors in a variety of contexts and explores the effects they have on states and security.

Playing on the title of Deborah Avant's early and important work on private security, *The Market for Force*, Dunigan and Petersohn expand to investigate multiple markets for force. They look not only at a range of state cases, and how these states both rely on and regulate private security, but more importantly, they propose a typology of different market types and identify three in the cases examined: neoliberal, hybrid, and racketeer. In the neoliberal market, based on profits and free competition, private firms are the main actors selling goods and services. The state is the main actor in the hybrid market, with "private" firms either owned or controlled by the state, or state forces offering services to clients other than the state. In some cases the goal is to produce revenues; in others, it is simply to sustain the military units that are marketing their services. Racketeer markets are dominated by criminal organizations or warlords with monopolies on force in delimited territories, who both sell security services and spread insecurity in order to increase demand.

Dunigan and Petersohn argue that different market types are caused by different factors, and they have different consequences with regard to the provision of security in two critical areas: the state's monopoly of the use of force and its provision of security as a public good. These are key measures of the state's ability and will to ensure the security of its citizens. Not surprisingly, racketeer markets are likely to affect these areas most negatively, and neoliberal markets have less harmful, though not necessarily positive, effects on the state's monopoly on force and provision of security as a public good. How the state exercises control over the market affects the outcome positively or negatively in hybrid markets.

The book begins with an introduction that lays out its goals and outlines the debate about causes for the emergence of private security markets. It then presents an analytic framework that specifies different possible market types, and seeks to illuminate their causes and consequences. Nine case studies follow, which cover twelve countries in Latin America, North America, Europe, and Asia, with variation in cultural factors and regime types. The editors are careful to note that this number is insufficient for comprehensive generalizations about possible market types or their frequency. The concluding chapter evaluates the explanatory power and implications of the market types, based on the case findings.

In the cases, the authors describe the markets that exist in different countries, laying out the providers and the nature of the services provided, as well as how these affect the state's monopoly on force and the provision of security as a public good. Some cases are well-known, such as the United Kingdom and the United States. Other chapters cover less familiar cases and help elucidate the variety in global private markets. In Latin America, for example, all three of the proposed market types exist, and security is provided in different states by both local and transnational private firms, criminal gangs, and local military units working for clients other than their government. Security is increasingly excludable rather than a public good, in spite of the spread of democracy in the region. China's market is dominated by domestic firms controlled by the state, but this is shifting with the state moving toward regulation and foreign firms seeking to compete more freely in the market. The Russian and Ukrainian markets are largely for export, based on informal networks and little regulation. The services offered are primarily aircraft pilots and armed guards, who contract with a broad range of clients for work in conflict zones.

The analysis leaves some gaps. Discussions of competing explanations feel cursory, and the analytic framework focused on market type does not address different levels of lethality or the distinction between domestic and external reliance on private security contractors satisfactorily. These matter to understanding the provision of security as a public good.

Overall, though, both the analytic framework and the case studies contribute to our understanding of the ways in which private security is managed, and the effects that different kinds of private actors have on states and citizens. The book is well-written and the arguments throughout are clear and concise. The book will be useful to both students and scholars interested in understanding the effects of security privatization.

Conscientious Objectors in Israel: Citizenship, Sacrifice, Trials of Fealty by Erica Weiss. Philadelphia: University of Pennsylvania Press, 2014 (216 pages; cloth).

Reviewed by Dan Lainer-Vos
University of California, Irvine

This book offers a comprehensive ethnographic study of conscientious objection in Israel. Weiss listens to the dilemmas of committed and prospective objectors, accompanies them in their activities, and examines the interactions between conscientious objectors, the public, and the state. Weiss structures the analysis between the opposing pillars of the liberal individualistic conception of consciousness, on the one hand, and the societal demand for military sacrifice, on the other. The result is a nuanced and theoretically informed account of one of the most interesting forms of activism in Israel today.

In the first two chapters, Weiss focuses on the experiences of the older generation of conscientious objectors, who are associated today with the Israeli-Palestinian "Combatants for Peace" movement. The Israeli members of Combatants for Peace served in the military in the past, often in elite combat units, and only later in life decided to refuse serving in the military or to refuse serving in the Occupied Territories. The dilemmas of the refusers, and the social reaction to their act, are marked by the recognition and honor associated with their past sacrifices.

The third chapter considers the experience of younger conscientious objectors who decided to refuse before ever enlisting. While the older generation of conscientious objectors effectively mobilizes their past military careers to garner sympathy and respect, younger objectors face sharp questioning and harsher sanctions. Chapter four continues this exploration by examining the interaction of young conscientious objectors with the military. Specifically, the chapter examines the work of the military's "Conscience Committee," the committee that grants exemption from military service to select objectors. The argument here is intriguing and tragic. Weiss convincingly demonstrates how, rather than recognizing conscientious objection as a principled choice, the committee defines pacifism in personal terms, as an involuntary aversion to all acts of violence. By treating conscientious objection as a personal incapacity, the committee pathologizes the conscientious objectors and frees the military from having to confront and debate the legitimacy of its actions.

Chapter five documents the consequences of refusal to serve in the military in Israel. Weiss shows how, in a society where military service is still considered as the ultimate sacrifice, the decision to refuse reverberates throughout the social space and ignites dormant tensions within families and among close friends.

Throughout the book, Weiss perceptively identifies delicate dynamics. Her analysis of the public work of Combatants for Peace is particularly intriguing. Combatants for Peace regularly organizes informational sessions for the public. In these events, members of the group describe the process that led to their refusal. While ostensibly framed as a "confession," the members of Combatants for Peace defy the public's expectation to hear about gross atrocities. Instead, they deliberately focus on the everyday routines involved in imposing military rule over a resisting population, the very routines most Israelis come to accept as unavoidable realities. By focusing on the ordinary aspects of the occupation, the members of the group effectively turn these confessional settings into a moment of sharp accusation, attempting to turn practices that most Israeli Jews accept as inoffensive into a crime.

Weiss organizes her analysis around the liberal conception of autonomous conscience. This conceptual choice requires some discussion. On the one hand, organizing the book around the theme of liberalism allows Weiss to escape the particularities of the Israeli case. But Israel can hardly be considered a liberal regime. Rather than defending the claim that the polity in Israel is liberal, Weiss's determination rests, above all, on the liberal framing and justification that conscientious objectors provide to their action. This is a problematic justification. First, it is not altogether clear from the evidence whether Weiss's subjects, especially the older generation of conscientious objectors, indeed espouse liberalism. Surely, they care about human rights, and see themselves as responsible right-bearing individuals, but they also have little hesitation when it comes to claiming privilege based on their military virtues. More pointedly, Weiss's analysis, especially in chapter four that analyzes the work of the military's Conscious Committee, moves beyond the perspective of the refusers, and identifies what she calls "the internal contradictions and limits of liberalism." (p. 108). In so doing, Weiss joins other critics of liberalism, a popular trend in today's anthropology, but the basis for this criticism is dubious since Israel's liberal credentials are highly contested. Overall, I am not sure that the emphasis on liberalism advances our understanding of the predicament that Israeli conscientious objectors face.

Sacrifice is another key theme. For instance, in describing the process that leads to refusal, Weiss shows that the members of Combatants for Peace were willing to sacrifice, but during their service in the Occupied Territories they become disillusioned. Instead of serving some moral common good, the state used their sacrifice primarily for the enforcement of military occupation over the Palestinians. In Weiss's terms, the refusers' well-intentioned sacrifice was interrupted. In this and other places in the text, Weiss deftly uses the myth of the binding of Isaac, which plays a central role in Israeli culture, to elucidate the special dilemmas of the refusers. I am highly sympathetic to the incorporation of sacrifice in the analysis. Previous works on conscientious objection and on war resistance in Israel more generally usually rely on the concept of citizenship. Citizenship touches upon the dynamic of sacrifice, but Weiss's analysis addresses it more explicitly and lucidly. Nevertheless, her conclusions are oversimplified and perhaps also naïve. Weiss does not oppose the logic of sacrifice per se, but she contends that "the state, necessarily guided by Realpolitik, should not be the object or organizer of sacrifice, because its creation of value will not be guided by ethical principles" (p. 168). Like many other modern polities, the Israeli polity effectively fuses nation and state and thus the object of sacrifice in Israel is not simply the state. More pointedly, given that we are dealing with the organization of violence, can there be a credible alternative to the state as the organizer of sacrifice? What would be the shape of a non-utopian solution to this problem of the sacrifice in this context? Weiss's analysis stops short of addressing this question.

———————— ■■■■■■■■■■■■■■■■■ ————————

Generation Vet: Composition, Student-Veterans, and the Post-9/11 University edited by Sue Doe and Lisa Langstraat. Logan, UT: Utah State University Press, 2014 (242 pages; paper).

Reviewed by Lisa Lebdusksa
Wheaton College, Massachusetts

The Veterans Educational Assistance Act of 2008, better known as the Post-9/11 G.I. Bill, is the most generous veterans benefits package since the original G.I. Bill, providing higher education to nearly one million veterans. This influx of veterans, like the one following World War II, promises to transform the educational landscape, inviting those who teach and administer higher education to reflect on what they do and how they can best reach a new student demographic. *Generation Vet: Composition, Student-Veterans, and the Post-9/11 University,* an anthology of essays about Post-9/11 student-veterans and the teaching of writing, offers valuable insights into how writing faculty and administrators can approach the competing values, rhetorical styles, and understandings of war, trauma, and military life that student-veterans bring to the college campus.

The editors—professors of composition at Colorado State University—have both personal and professional experience with the US military. Sue Doe, the daughter of a World War II veteran and the wife of a retired US Army lieutenant colonel, and Lisa Langstraat, daughter of a retired US Army chief warrant officer, have edited a wide-ranging collection of essays by student-veterans, teacher-veterans, and teacher-civilians, as well as some who wear multiple hats. The book recognizes the diversity of veteran experience and takes pains to offer a balanced view that neither romanticizes nor demonizes the student-veteran through clear-eyed views on how student-veterans are affecting the educational landscape, what they bring to the classroom, and what faculty and administrators can do to respond this changing altering terrain.

The editors have grouped fifteen essays into three sections: "Beyond the Military-Civilian Divide: Understanding Veterans," "Veterans and Public Audiences," and "Veteran-Friendly Composition Practices." The essays come from a variety of genres ranging from narratives that draw heavily on autobiographical accounts to more qualitative analyses like Ann Shivers-McNair's "A New Mission: Veteran-Led Learning Communities in the Basic Writing Classroom" and Corrine E. Hinton's "'Front and Center': Marine Student-Veterans, Collaboration, and the Writing Center." Taken together, these essays stake out central issues in writing and student-veteran education, including the cultivation of agency; the place of the personal narrative; teacher and student responses to both posttraumatic stress disorder (PTSD) and traumatic brain injury (TBI); and the role of veterans-only writing classes and non-academic writing spaces in veteran education, acculturation, and healing.

The editors and contributors agree that there is no single "veteran" profile and yet, as Angie Mallory and Doug Downs, the contributors of "Uniform Meets Rhetoric: Excellence through Interaction" observe, the military manages to train thousands of individuals from diverse backgrounds, abilities, and perspectives in such a way that they "respond uniformly and automatically in intense life-or-death situations" (p. 59). At the same time, while the military inculcates an adherence to authority and the necessity of obeying orders, it nevertheless recognizes extreme moments in the heat of battle when individuals must abandon predetermined scripts in order to save lives (the authors cite Medal of Honor recipient Sgt. Dakota Meyer as an example). The military training that shapes individuals into high-performing groups depends on hierarchy and clear directives—qualities that may conflict with nonhierarchical, inquiry-driven composition pedagogies that foster a certain degree of ambiguity and cognitive dissonance designed to cultivate independent thinking and flexible approaches to writing contexts. Mallory and Downs draw on James Paul Gee's theories of discourse to explain and respond to the tension that emerged in their own classroom as student-veteran and teacher respectively, concluding that student-veterans are learning a new discourse and scripts that include new models of leadership and learning. For them, continuous feedback for student and instructor alike, as well as ongoing transparency, facilitate education.

The teaching of composition has always involved an artful blend of recognizing the individual in light of social, political, and disciplinary forces, and there is no consensus within the field itself over the extent to which the composition classroom is a space for personal narratives, or to what extent individuals can or should first be taught to find their voices before moving on to engage with the voices, ideas, and perspectives of other individuals or social or political structures. Several of the essays engage these issues in terms of trauma and the student-veteran and teacher preparedness in dealing with trauma-focused narratives. Linda S. De La Ysla's "Faculty as First Responders: Willing but Unprepared," for example, offers a candid, complex account of her attempts to support a student who wrote about his battle experiences. Several contributors challenge the stereotype of the traumatized student-veteran, while also acknowledging that, for the student-veteran who does suffer from PTSD, writing can offer therapeutic benefits. Roger Thompson, however, cautions about using the composition classroom for such writing. In "Recognizing Silence: Composition, Writing, and the Ethical Space for War" he points out that given complex class dynamics, the classroom may be an "unsafe venue" for writing about trauma (p. 206). Allowing silence to be a choice and therefore a strategy for dealing with stress and or difference, he argues, may be the best approach. In some cases, veteran students may be better served by composing personal narratives outside the classroom. Eileen E. Schell and Ivy Kleinbart explain the benefits of self-sponsored writing as they describe their writing center-based veterans writing group at Syracuse University.

The editors are to be commended for the balanced perspective the essays take: no program is offered as the sole solution to promoting learning. As with most inclusive education, the strategies offered here would benefit any population: writing assignment choice, faculty understanding of students as individuals, and clear communication of goals and expectations. And, as both Doe and Langstraat note, there is still much to be discovered about student-veteran education. This collection has laid the groundwork for asking about what can and should come next.

———————— • • • • • • • • • • • • • • • ————————

The American Way of Bombing: Changing Ethical and Legal Norms, From Flying Fortresses to Drones edited by Matthew Evangelista and Henry Shue. Ithaca: Cornell University Press, 2014 (328 pages; paper).

Reviewed by Valerie Morkevičius
Colgate University

Matthew Evangelista and Henry Shue's edited volume, *The American Way of Bombing,* provides an excellent overview of the evolving norms governing the American use of airpower from the initial development of strategic air war theory in the interwar years to the emerging norms governing the contemporary use of cluster munitions and drones. The book's real strength is the historical focus of its first two sections, which admirably demonstrate that, in many ways, what is old is new again. Our concerns about air war's effects on civilians—and our justifications for overriding those concerns—have changed remarkably little. Read together, the book's essays build a compelling argument suggesting that restraint emerges when ethical norms and strategic beliefs coincide.

As Tami Davis Biddle and Neta Crawford point out in their essays, early air war doctrine presumed that attack from the air would sow "disruption and panic," undermining civilians' political and economic support for the war effort (pp. 27, 68). Later, Biddle demonstrates that this assumption has proven durable despite clear evidence from World War II that civilians respond to bombings not with panic but with anger. Thus, Richard W. Miller finds that, even during the first Gulf War, "grave damage to civilian lives through destruction of Iraqi infrastructure was regarded as a possible way to deprive Saddam Hussein of support and encourage his overthrow" (p. 162). Similarly, Charles J. Dunlap Jr. asserts that "experience shows that the erosion of the 'will' of an adversary through the *indirect* effects of aerial bombardment on civilians is a key element of victory in modern war" (p. 116). When coupled with an urgent need to win against a powerful advisory, this assumption leads to devastating bombings of civilian areas, as witnessed not only in World War II but also in Korea and in the first Linebacker campaign in Vietnam.

And yet, in a seeming contradiction, Miller demonstrates that American leaders—and the public as well—have consistently voiced commitment to a norm *against* targeting civilians directly. Truman famously described the dropping of the A-bomb on Hiroshima as an attack on a "Japanese army base" (p. 161). Likewise, during the Korean War, American military and political leaders claimed that civilians were never the intended targets, despite the fact that vast "parts of civilian society behind the front line were deemed a vital component of a war effort," including industrial sites and transportation hubs, as Sahr Conway-Lanz reveals (p. 61). Today, the "increased public scrutiny made possible by embedded journalists, social media, and a 24-hour news cycle" has made the "reputational costs of inflicting death and destruction . . . higher than they ever were in human history," which Janina Dill argues adds to the pressure on military planners (p. 139).

Given the tension between strategic beliefs and ethical norms, efforts to restrain airpower to protect civilians must appeal to both simultaneously. After all, when strategic and ethical interests coincide, as they do in humanitarian interventions and counterinsurgency campaigns, Crawford argues that the United States tends to exercise considerable restraint. Any new ethico-legal regime hoping to be effective in protecting civilians must make allowances for military necessity, including force protection, as Henry Shue makes clear. Thus, Charles Garraway suggests that the tendency to push for the application of human rights law (rather than humanitarian law) to certain non-international conflicts—particularly high intensity ones such as those in Iraq or Afghanistan—is misdirected. NGOs can also use this overlap between strategic and ethical concerns to encourage states to adopt new protections for civilians, as Margarita H. Petrova reveals.

The volume's final essays, exploring drone warfare, would be more compelling if they incorporated this rich history. By focusing on how drones "scramble" space and time, leading to a dissociation of agents and targets, Hugh Gusterson and Klem Ryan's otherwise strong contributions fail to recognize the deep parallels between the drone debate and earlier ethical debates about airpower. Indeed, the shift to drone warfare seems driven by the same political and strategic pressures that led to the initial rise of precision airpower: the public's demand for the protection of deployed forces *and* enemy civilians in the context of asymmetric conflicts, where winning hearts and minds matters strategically. Even the physical distance between the inflictors of violence and their victims is not so revolutionary—as the book's earlier essays reveal, similar concerns have been present since the beginning of air war.

By contrast, the development of fully autonomous weapons systems that would exercise lethal force without a human in the loop is truly revolutionary. Nonetheless, some lessons from the volume's earlier chapters remain applicable. Mary Ellen O'Connell argues that autonomous drones should be banned outright, just as blinding lasers were in the past. Blinding lasers, unlike drones, were not seen as strategically valuable, making such a ban palatable. If the past is prologue, any hope of limiting the development of autonomous weapons systems must rely not only on ethical arguments but also on strategic ones as well.

In This Issue

Constantine P. Danopoulos is Professor of Political Science and President's Scholar at San José State University. He served as department chair and received the Warburton Award for Excellence in Research. In addition he has been a visiting scholar at the University of Paris, Belgrano University, as well as other institutions of higher learning in South Korea and elsewhere. A former Fulbright Scholar to Greece, he has authored or edited eleven books and over seventy journal articles and book chapters on national security, civil-military relations, bureaucracy, poverty, democratic consolidation, and the quality of democracy. His work has been published in *Armed Forces and Society, Political Science Quarterly, West European Politics, Mediterranean Quarterly,* and *Third World Quarterly.* He was an election observer in Bosnia and has served as president of the Research Committee on Armed Forces and Society of the International Political Science Association and as editor of the *Journal of Political and Military Sociology.*

Ifeanyi Ezeonu is Associate Professor of Sociology and Criminology at Brock University. He has research interests and has published on organized crime and violent armed groups (including youth gangs), critical security studies, the political economy of crime, economic justice, and the contemporary African Diaspora. He is a coeditor of *Remembering Biafra: Narrative, History and Memory of the Nigeria-Biafra War.*

Remi M. Hajjar is an Academy Professor, Associate Professor, and the Sociology Program Director in the Department of Behavioral Sciences and Leadership at the United States Military Academy. Military sociology, cultural sociology, leadership, and education constitute his major fields of research and publication. His academic affiliations include the American Sociological Association, the Inter-University Seminar on Armed Forces and Society, the Eastern Sociological Society, the North Central Sociological Association, and the Proteus Futures

Working Group. He has served numerous leadership, staff, instructor, and professor assignments at Schofield Barracks, Hawaii; Fort Huachuca, Arizona; the United States Military Academy; the International Security Assistance Force in Kabul, Afghanistan; and the Multinational Security and Transition Command in Baghdad, Iraq.

Andreas Krieg is Assistant Professor in the Defence Studies Department at King's College London. He is currently working for the Qatari Armed Forces in their local Staff College in Doha. His research has focused on security studies with special focus on the Middle East. Currently, he is completing a book on the changing nature of civil-security sector relations in the region. Having lived in the Middle East for many years, he provides strategic risk consultancy and analysis on regional affairs for governmental organizations, commercial clients, and the media.

Godfrey Maringira is a Volkswagen Stiftung Postdoctoral Fellow based at the University of the Western Cape, where he earned his PhD in sociology. He has conducted research on South African ex-combatants, funded by the International Development Research Center and the African Peacebuilding Network (Carnegie Corporation). His main research areas include the ethnography of war, soldiers and the environment, African army deserters, and the military in post colonial Africa. He has published in *Armed Forces & Society* and *Sociology.*